T0188130

Embracing Chatbots in Higher Education

This book explores the integration of AI-powered chatbots such as ChatGPT into higher education for instructional and communication purposes. The author emphasizes the responsibility of higher education institutions to equip students with advanced skills for writing with AI assistance, and prepare them for an increasingly AI-driven world.

Offering numerous practical tips, the book demonstrates how universities can increase student success, and stem the rising cost of higher education by employing AI tools. The chapters discuss streamlining tasks such as grading, providing feedback, and handling administrative duties, to show how educators can be enabled to focus on more meaningful aspects of their work. The author also reflects on the philosophical and ethical considerations and potential pitfalls of relying on AI in higher education, including concerns about academic integrity and the importance of human input in the learning process. The author offers a responsible and informed approach to incorporating the new powerful tools into the academic landscape.

This volume will be a key resource for higher education faculty and administrators seeking to navigate the complex intersection of AI and writing.

Alexander M. Sidorkin is Chief AI Officer at California State University, Sacramento, USA.

Routledge Research in Digital Education and Educational Technology

This series provides a forum for established and emerging scholars to discuss the latest debates, research and practice in the field of digital education and educational technology globally, including distance and open learning.

Credit: Artwork by Svetlana N. Sidorkina

Embracing Chatbots in Higher Education

The Use of Artificial Intelligence in Teaching, Administration, and Scholarship

Alexander M. Sidorkin

NEW YORK AND LONDON

First published 2024
by Routledge
605 Third Avenue, New York, NY 10158

and by Routledge
4 Park Square, Milton Park, Abingdon, Oxon, OX14 4RN

Routledge is an imprint of the Taylor & Francis Group, an informa business

ISBN: 978-1-032-68597-7 (hbk)
ISBN: 978-1-032-68601-1 (pbk)
ISBN: 978-1-032-68602-8 (ebk)

DOI: 10.4324/9781032686028

Typeset in Times New Roman
by Apex CoVantage, LLC

Contents

Acknowledgments

I am grateful to the members of a professional learning community at Sacramento State's College of Education who helped me to start thinking about the use of AI in higher education: Frank Adamson, Susan Baker, Chris Boosalis, Basia Ellis, Elizabeth Ferry-Perata, Sue Hobbs, Alicia Herrera, Jessica Martinez, Patrick Pieng, Binod Pokhrel, Sheeva Sabati, and Mei Shen.

1 The Fundamentals

Introduction: The Age of "Wraiting"

Recently, I found myself coordinating an international academic conference. A request for a certificate of participation came in from a Greek participant. This is a common document within Greek academia, but a concept somewhat foreign to North America. A year ago, this would have meant scouring Google for examples and then laboriously drafting the certificate myself, an unappealing and time-consuming task. However, in 2023, I had the luxury of delegating this task to ChatGPT.

All that was required from my end was to copy and paste the participant's name and presentation title from our program and a brief description of the conference from our website. Everything else was handled by ChatGPT. Within a mere ten minutes, the certificate was generated, refined, and sent out—a staggering increase in efficiency of 83%. One of the first studies of productivity gains from ChatGPT shows that, for mid-level professional writing tasks, the time spent decreases by 40% while quality rises by 18%.[1] Those are very impressive numbers.

If you find it easy to dismiss this degree of efficiency gains as unworthy of exploration, then it is best to close this book now. There is little I could offer to sway your conviction. However, if you find such a prospect intriguing, I invite you to read on. This book will explore the transformative potential of AI in writing-related tasks for academic contexts. It will discuss how to navigate its challenges, and present a guide on how to integrate this technology responsibly and equitably into higher education.

The advent of the AI era introduces "wraiting," which is simply writing with the help of AI. It can also be called AI-assisted writing. If harnessed effectively, it can foster a synergy between human creativity and the unbridled computational power of AI. This novel practice presents a fascinating set of opportunities and challenges that are as intriguing as they are significant, compelling us to delve deep into the enthralling realm of wraiting.

This book postulates that wraiting is an advanced skill. Now, you might be thinking: why is something meant to *simplify* writing being presented as a

DOI: 10.4324/9781032686028-1

complex skill? Well, *all* tools designed to make our lives easier require understanding and skills to use effectively. Different people are adept at using different tools; some might be proficient with Adobe Photoshop, while others might be skilled with a race car or a violin. This great diversity of skills owes its existence to the need for specialized knowledge in every line of work.

The same pattern applies to this new tool, the AI-powered chatbot. It is undoubtedly easy to use. Simply go online, set up an account, and start typing or pasting your questions or requests. That is the beginning and end of the user manual: type or paste a question or request and press "Enter." Compared to other information-technology innovations, this one has a remarkably low threshold for the initial use. However, using it to produce high-quality texts while also saving significant time is not so straightforward. While I do not consider myself a world champion in using AI-powered chatbots, my skills are better than those of most of my colleagues. As an educator and academic leader, I appreciate the trends, recognize the potential of this new tool, and understand its implications for higher education.

However, another question emerges: is it worth investing time in mastering the more advanced uses of this new tool? Each person must answer this for themselves. I encourage pragmatism over prejudice. Try it first, and form an opinion later. Specifically, for educators and administrators, I see several compelling reasons to either invest time or at least consider the insights of this book:

1. Students are bound to use it, both in school and beyond. We should prepare them for the workplace of the future, not the one of today.
2. "Wraiting" is much faster than traditional writing once you get the hang of it.
3. The quality of output may improve for many people and for most kinds of text.

Indeed, there are compelling reasons to invest the time, particularly if your professional role revolves around professional communications, scholarship, and teaching. Change is inevitable, and resistance to innovation can be costly to educators. Most importantly, it can be costly to our students. Resistance is driven by various factors, ranging from imminent retirement to an ideological stance. It is known from the earliest innovation studies that adoption of innovations is never uniform or simultaneous.[2] However, this particular innovation will be adopted quickly, because of the tremendous pressure from employers and students themselves. Its disruptive potential is very strong, and we in higher education may not have a choice in the matter.

Normally, I tend to hold off on learning new digital tools until I am convinced of their worth. There have been many tools that generated much hype, only to fade into the background. In the mid-2000s, a new technology, called "clickers" or audience response systems, created a wave of excitement in the world of education. They were touted as revolutionary tools that would make classes, especially large lectures, more interactive by allowing real-time, instant feedback. Schools invested heavily in these devices, and educational conferences buzzed with discussions about their potential. However, over time, the initial enthusiasm faded. Educators found that clickers did not themselves improve teaching or engagement. Instead, their effectiveness was tied to the quality of the pedagogical strategies employed. Additionally, logistical issues and the rise of multifunctional smartphones rendered these standalone devices redundant. By the late 2010s, the hype around clickers had largely dissipated, teaching us that any new technology by itself is not a panacea, but merely a tool whose value is intrinsically tied to its application. This is just one example of the "tool fetishism"[3] that is so typical for education technology.

With AI-powered chatbots, we are facing a phenomenon of a different order of magnitude. It represents a radical shift, larger than the transition from early search engines to Google, and larger than the introduction of word processing software. If you are old enough to remember these two, you can appreciate the scale of this change.

However, the decision to incorporate AI into our teaching practices should be a mindful, deliberate choice. To choose to do or not to do something, one needs to have a full picture of the option that is being embraced or rejected. In other words, if you know nothing about the use of AI in writing, your choice to reject is uninformed and arbitrary. That is another reason to learn about it.

This book is intended to help understand potential applications of AI-powered text-based tools in higher education. It is organized into five chapters: the first provides an overview of the fundamentals, while the subsequent chapters delve into the application of AI chatbots in three major domains: teaching, scholarship, and professional communications. The final chapter navigates ethical and philosophical considerations.

Most of my experience lies with OpenAI's ChatGPT model 4, the pioneering platform that unleashed the era of AI onto the mass market. I have also spent significant time with Claude 2, released in July of 2023.[4] Unlike its predecessor, which was not intended for mass use, Claude 2 can process much longer text inputs than ChatGPT. However, it appears less consistent in output quality and has a slower response time. As I will demonstrate throughout the book, some tasks are better handled by Claude, and others by ChatGPT. I utilize both daily, often in tandem, using the output of one to construct a prompt for the other.

I have also explored Google's Bard, another AI chatbot that operates similarly to ChatGPT. Bard's constraints, particularly concerning the length of text it can generate, may limit its utility in certain scenarios, especially for longer-form content. Google has also integrated a limited AI capability into its Google Docs interface, allowing text within a document to be rewritten, or edited. While this is a promising and convenient interface that eliminates the need for multiple copying and pasting, the quality of its output is still behind that of the major competitors.

Microsoft's Bing chatbot stands out with its real-time data access, distinguishing it from many counterparts. However, its utility for writing tasks seems less substantial compared to ChatGPT, Claude, or Bard. It might be better described as a supplement to a typical search engine rather than a full-fledged language-generating chatbot, with its strength lying more in data retrieval than creative writing or text generation. At present, ChatGPT is the most robust model in this field, although this status is by no means permanent. Claude's unique ability to process extended inputs offers a promising direction for future development.

The bottom line in the rapidly evolving AI landscape is that ChatGPT's influence has sparked promising innovations, but its long-term dominance is far from guaranteed. This competition should eventually lead to enhanced AI capabilities for consumers, but it is wise to temper expectations. It may take years of refinement and shifts in regulatory environments before any single contender can claim the title in the AI realm.

This book serves as an initial investigation into the rapidly emerging field of AI-powered chatbots and their potential applications in higher education. Because these consumer-oriented technologies are still relatively new, there is a lack of extensive research and established best practices for their use. However, the potential for significant impact makes immediate study essential. To understand this phenomenon effectively, it is crucial to accumulate substantial experience using AI in higher education. This book aims to accelerate the accumulation of such practical experience so that it can be studied more rigorously.

My approach invites readers to participate in a shared experiment, exploring this uncharted domain through hands-on experiences rather than controlled studies. Rather than a trove of proven solutions, this book serves as an initial "treasure map," pinpointing promising areas for exploration. It compiles hints, insights, and findings from my numerous micro-experiments in daily interactions with chatbots.

Though light on citations due to the emerging nature of the field, this discovery-based approach sets the stage for future research by providing essential practical understanding. As we collectively uncover the benefits and effective applications of AI technology through shared experiences, we can move toward a future where AI chatbots enhance the field of higher education.

The Rich Prompt

In this section, I will present the concept of the "rich prompt"—the key ingredient in our recipe for successful "wraiting."

One of the primary benefits of AI is that it does not ask us to master a distinct language to communicate with it. This has historically been, and continues to be, a steep barrier to using computers. While we have significantly moved away from the era of punch cards, interacting with a piece of software still requires us to learn its unique menus, interfaces, and conventions.

The AI-powered chatbot is designed to understand natural language, even if it is not expressed perfectly clearly. You can pose a direct question to it or ask it to generate a certain piece of text based on what you provide. However, there are better or worse questions or requests, and they will produce very different responses.

Let us commence with an essential reality check: AI does not possess the capability to "think" in the same way that humans do. It is best perceived as an amplifier for our thoughts, rather than an independent generator of ideas. It also can find and present ideas already expressed by others. The power of AI lies not in autonomous creation, but rather in the realms of effective communication and enhancement of ideas presented to it.

When using AI, especially in contexts such as language generation, the quality of the output is intrinsically tied to the quality of the input. In other words, if you provide it with what I call a "lazy prompt," you are likely to receive a mediocre or non-specific reply—this is often summed up as "garbage in—garbage out." Sometimes the garbage looks fine at first glance. But read it more carefully, and you will see it is still just neatly packaged garbage.

What I refer to as a "lazy prompt" is the act of pasting a task into a chatbot without any modification or additional guidance. Essentially, this is when you are not adding any personal input to the task. For example, a student might directly copy an essay assignment from a syllabus and paste it into a chatbot like ChatGPT, expecting a high-quality output. In the vast majority of situations, this kind of lazy prompting yields unsatisfactory results.

However, there are rare instances where a lazy prompt might be justifiable. For example, if you are dealing with a bureaucratic task that you deem entirely meaningless, a lazy prompt might suffice for that specific context. But in most other scenarios you will need to invest your own thoughts or perspectives into the prompt to produce content that is actually valuable or meaningful. The key takeaway is that quality output usually requires quality input; you have to give a little to get something worthwhile in return.

Conversely, when presented with a rich, well-crafted prompt, AI has the potential to generate something extraordinary, or at least deeply satisfying. It can weave together vast amounts of information, providing insights or compositions that might have taken much longer for a human to construct. Understanding the strengths and limitations of AI as a powerful tool, rather than an independent thinker, can enable us to utilize it more effectively in a multitude of applications.

Crafting rich prompts is an art, one that varies with context. Yet, despite their diversity, successful prompts share common elements. Let us delve into what constitutes a "rich" prompt, and how you can master the art of "wraiting."

The art of the rich prompt can be boiled down to these five points: give it an idea, give it a job, give it some food, give it a genre, and give it another push. Note that not every prompt has to meet all these criteria. In fact, you will see that a skillful use of conversations can reduce the prompts to a minimum. "Rich" does not mean "long." It indicates quality, not quantity. Yet every good conversation with an AI-powered chatbot will start with a rich prompt.

Give It an Idea

A rich prompt begins with a novel, unique idea that challenges AI to explore new avenues of thought. The more original and thought-provoking the idea, the more innovative and insightful the AI's response is likely to be.

AI models demonstrate proficiency in predicting likely sequences of text, adeptly encapsulating, and conveying widely accepted ideas. However, they consistently fall short of innovative thinking—an area traditionally within the purview of human intellect. Consequently, the first fundamental principle when using an AI chatbot is to recognize that the task of ideation—the birth of fresh concepts and content—remains squarely in the human domain, even though your own creativity may be stimulated by something AI generates.

In fact, if you encounter an output that presents something previously unknown to you, it is quite likely that it is reflecting existing knowledge of which you were simply unaware. It is true that AI can sometimes be nudged to inject a degree of randomness into its output, and, indeed, randomness can contribute an element of novelty. The degree to which novelty is attributed to randomness is a complex issue, which we will not delve into here. But it is important to remember that a well-presented point is not the same thing as an original idea, even though people routinely confuse the two.

The tendency to conflate thinking and expression can potentially skew our understanding of these distinct processes. Thinking frequently occurs independently of linguistic expression. Some individuals might excel at articulating thoughts but struggle when it comes to creating original ideas. The rise of AI-assisted writing can expose these weaknesses more prominently. One potential impact of the widespread use of chatbots could be that we will eventually sharpen our ability to differentiate between eloquent writing and original thought. Recognizing this distinction is a vital skill in both using AI tools effectively and appraising the intellectual contributions of others accurately.

Let us be real with ourselves: not all writing calls for originality. When it comes to the art of crafting prompts, context is king. Think back to that certificate of participation example from our introduction; it did not require any earth-shattering ideas. In fact, much of our professional or academic communications does not demand a spark of creative thinking. Instead, it calls for alignment with established norms and conventions. Think of memos or reports—they are not typically vessels for groundbreaking concepts. In situations where compliance is paramount, being too original can, strangely enough, become a hurdle. But that is perfectly alright; it is simply the nature of those particular writing tasks.

Regardless of the genre, whether it is a memo, an email, a report, or a piece of creative writing, it is essential to have a tight grip on the main idea or message you are looking to convey. Understanding your intent will help you craft powerful prompts and, in turn, extract the most value from your AI tool. So, even if your writing does not call for original thought, clarity of purpose remains critical. That is the secret sauce to making AI work for you!

Give It a Job

Setting up the "job" for an AI chatbot is a crucial step in achieving the desired results. Simply put, it is not just about giving the AI an idea; it is also about defining the work it has to do with that idea. You need to provide it with clear instructions and set it on a specific course.

If you are drafting a scholarly article and need the AI to help improve your writing, a task could be "correct grammatical errors." Here, you are clearly directing the AI to focus on grammar, to review your writing for errors, and to correct them. This task ensures that the AI does not stray into irrelevant territory, such as critiquing your argument or rearranging your logic.

Alternatively, you might want the AI to enrich your text with examples and metaphors. In this case, the task could be "expand with more examples and metaphors." This prompt guides the AI to not only stick to your idea but also support it with additional examples and metaphors, making your argument more vivid and engaging.

Finally, suppose you are involved in a debate and need the AI to help you think of counterarguments. The task could be "provide counterarguments to . . ." This request assigns the AI the job of thinking critically about your position and formulating plausible counterarguments.

In each of these examples, the task you set significantly impacts the output from the AI. Active verbs such as "correct," "expand," and "provide" clarify the job for the AI, leading to a more focused and useful response. They constitute a necessary part of a rich prompt, leading to a more specific, appropriate, and helpful output from the AI.

Starting with short paragraphs and specific ideas when writing with AI can be an effective strategy for generating high-quality content. To make the most of this approach, it can be helpful to use a range of productive prompts that encourage deeper thinking and more detailed analysis.

Try using active verbs to describe the job you want AI to do for you, for example:

1. Elaborate: One useful prompt is to ask the AI to elaborate on specific points or ideas in your text. For example, you could ask the AI to expand on a particular argument or to provide more details about a concept. This can help you to flesh out your ideas and ensure that your content is comprehensive and well-developed.
2. Support by providing additional arguments: Another productive prompt is to ask the AI to provide additional arguments or evidence in support of your

main ideas. This can help you to build a more persuasive case and ensure that your content is backed up by solid research and analysis.

3. Support by citing specific research: To further strengthen your arguments, you can ask the AI to provide specific research or studies that support your claims. This can help you to add credibility to your content and demonstrate that you have done your homework.

4. Illustrate with additional examples: Another useful prompt is to ask the AI to provide additional examples or case studies that illustrate your main points. This can help you to make your content more engaging and relatable to your readers.

5. Provide analogies to elaborate: Analogies can be a powerful tool for explaining complex ideas in a more relatable way. You can ask the AI to provide analogies or metaphors that help to clarify your main points and make them more accessible to your audience.

6. Present a counterargument to this: To ensure that your content is well-rounded and comprehensive, it can be helpful to ask the AI to provide counterarguments to your main points. This can help you to identify potential objections and weaknesses in your arguments and address them proactively in your content.

7. Clarify/elucidate: If you find that your text is unclear or confusing, you can ask the AI to clarify specific points or ideas. For example, you could ask the AI to rephrase a sentence or to explain a concept in simpler terms.

8. Summarize: To ensure that your content is easy to understand and digest, you can ask the AI to summarize specific sections or ideas. This can help you to condense complex information into a more concise and readable format.

9. Evaluate or critique: If you are unsure about the quality or effectiveness of your writing, you can ask the AI to evaluate specific sections or the overall piece. The AI could provide feedback on the tone, style, or clarity of your writing, or suggest ways to improve your arguments or presentation.

10. Generate: Another useful prompt is to ask the AI to generate new ideas or content related to your topic. This can help you to explore new angles or perspectives on your subject matter and come up with fresh insights or approaches.

11. Compare and contrast: If you are exploring multiple ideas or approaches, you can ask the AI to compare and contrast them. This can help you to identify the strengths and weaknesses of different arguments or strategies and determine which one is most effective.

12. Predict: If you are writing about a topic that involves future trends or developments, you can ask the AI to make predictions or projections. The AI could draw on data and trends to make informed guesses about what might happen in the future.

The best help with AI is provided by AI itself. For example, it is always a good idea to use specific verbs while assigning a task. I was not sure how it interprets the difference between "elucidate" and "expand." Instead of experimenting with actual text, it is just easier to ask it. And here is the response:

> When you use the command "elucidate," I interpret it as a request to make something clearer, more understandable, or to provide further explanation on a particular point. The aim is to clarify the original meaning without necessarily adding much more content. It often involves explaining complex terms, providing additional context, or rephrasing for improved clarity.
>
> On the other hand, "expand" implies that you want me to add more information, detail, or breadth to the original content. It involves going beyond the initial statement, providing additional details, examples, or related information that could make the point more comprehensive or thorough.

Note that ChatGPT and other chatbots understand repetition of prompts. If you want the same operation with the next fragment of test, just say "do the same with this . . . ." After a few repetitions, just paste the next segment without any prompt whatsoever.

Give It Some Food

The practice of "wraiting" thrives on details, and, as such, it is necessary to feed the AI with ample information. Here, "Give it some food" is a metaphor that underscores the necessity of enriching your prompts.

As you venture into the realm of AI-assisted writing, you may find that a sentence or two is simply not enough. Single sentences can be ambiguous, leading to outputs that may not align with your intent. On the other hand, rich prompts, akin to full paragraphs, paint a comprehensive picture of what you expect from the AI. They enable the AI to better understand the context, thereby reducing the chance of misinterpretation and increasing the likelihood of producing the desired response. If you are writing a blog with three points, list all three points, and beef them up with some detail. It is not always important which specific details, an example, or a hint will make the output better.

In administrative communications, recycling existing texts as part of your prompt can often be a strategic approach to crafting effective communication. I will give more examples and guidance in Chapter Four. This does not mean copying and pasting text indiscriminately, but rather curating snippets that can guide the AI in the right direction. Whether it is a set of key points from a past report or snippets from well-received presentations, these texts can serve as a blueprint, helping the AI grasp the style, tone, and content you desire. Claude is especially adept at devouring large texts from which it can then harvest both contextual and factual information. Claude's interface allows for file attachments, which I consider to be parts of the prompt. In ChatGPT, one needs to paste any "food" into the same prompt window. Keep in mind that ChatGPT will not process more than 2000 pasted words total in one prompt, so you may need to be more selective about how much it can swallow at one time. However, there is a way around it by uploading files.

To illustrate, let us consider a situation where you are crafting a grant proposal. You could incorporate extracts from a previous successful proposal, effectively training the AI on the desired structure, key points to include, perhaps borrowed from one of your publications, or from an email you write to your collaborator, and the tone that resonates with your audience. AI is omnivorous and will take everything into consideration. This way, you are not starting from scratch, but using established texts as scaffolding for new, yet consistent, content.

Avoid the pitfall of excessive brevity and instead provide a comprehensive base for the AI to work from. By doing so, you will be setting the stage for the creation of content that is not only contextually accurate but also resonates with your target audience.

Give It a Genre

In the quest to master the art of creating a rich prompt, the importance of specifying your audience, style, and genre cannot be overstated. This triumvirate forms the contextual backbone of your prompt, guiding the AI to tailor its output accordingly.

Your audience could range from a group of corporate executives to middle school students, and their backgrounds, understanding, and interests significantly influence the kind of content that will resonate with them. A pointer to the AI on who the audience is can thus significantly enhance the relevance and effectiveness of the generated content. For instance, a report for a business audience may need to be filled with industry jargons, while an academic paper may demand a more scholarly language.

The style of your content serves to refine the AI's approach, determining the voice and tone of the written piece. For instance, a formal business report requires a professional and authoritative style, while a creative narrative may call for a more informal, expressive tone. By providing clear stylistic instructions to the AI, you ensure that the generated text aligns with your expectations, whether you desire a somber, humorous, casual, or scholarly tone.

In many cases, a brief description is enough to guide the AI. Typing commands like "write a blog" or "write a memo" will shift the output style to be more conversational or formal, respectively.

Furthermore, the genre acts as the framework for your content, defining its structure and conventions. Each type, whether it is a scientific research paper, business proposal, or fiction story, carries its own set of rules and expectations. Specifying the genre in your prompt helps the AI adhere to these conventions, ensuring the output is consistent with the norms of the chosen genre.

The AI language models have a remarkable understanding of various text genres, thanks to their training on an extensive range of texts, including academic papers, emails, blog posts, and memos. Through this exposure, the models can discern the unique language patterns, structures, and conventions associated with each genre. As a result, AI can generate a text that precisely aligns with the specific genre you need. This ability is especially valuable in diverse writing scenarios, as it aids in shaping your writing to meet the conventions of the target genre.

Give It a Push

Crafting a rich prompt is not a one-shot deal; it is often an iterative process. When you receive the AI's response, take a moment to consider it, and then refine your prompt based on the outcome. This could involve further clarification of the task, adding more detail, adjusting the tone, or even pivoting the idea. This is the interaction between you and the AI—an ongoing exchange that brings the most effective content to life. You can ask the chatbot to redo, with adding new conditions, or you can revise the original prompt, and submit it again.

Improving your prompt is a skill, as delicate as any art form, which does not allow for shortcuts or simple recipes. It calls for practice, experimentation, and constant fine-tuning. As we step into the realm of AI-assisted writing, it is important to accept the unpredictability of AI-generated content. There is a black box between your input and the output, to which you have no access. The only way to improve quality is to tweak the input. The advanced skill lies not in memorizing a set of great prompts, but in the ability to improvise and refine prompts based on quick evaluation of the output.

When the AI's output falls short of your expectations, revise the prompt. Is it clear? Does it have enough detail? Refining a less-than-perfect prompt could be the key to obtaining satisfactory results. However, if a well-crafted prompt still fails to yield the desired output, it might be an indication that the subject matter is an unfamiliar territory for the AI, or it got confused within the conversation.

In such cases, consider it as an opportunity to engage in original writing, rather than a frustration. By acknowledging AI's limitations and seizing the chance to add our unique perspectives, we can leverage AI's strengths to create work that is both innovative and engaging. As we continue to merge human creativity with AI, the evolving relationship between the writer and AI will open exciting new possibilities in writing.

The AI-enhanced writing process introduces a unique dynamic to this practice. The AI serves as a real-time feedback mechanism, offering insights and suggestions for refining prompts. As this interplay continues to evolve, we might see AI systems determining the best prompts for generating high-quality content, thereby refining their feedback mechanism to enhance the output. You can query, "How effective is my prompt? What additional information do you need to improve the output?" Often, the AI will provide a sensible recommendation.

I must highlight the fact that honing your skills in crafting prompts can be a significant boost for your growth not only as a "wraiter," but also as a writer. As you continue refining your prompts, you will learn to differentiate more astutely between ideas and their expression. This practice compels you to be more precise and focused on your central message or concept, sharpening your skill in conveying your thoughts with clarity. This is exactly why we in higher education should not only learn the skill of "wraiting" but also teach it to our students.

Third-party Plug-ins

As we reach the conclusion of the discussion of rich prompts, I want to highlight the rapidly growing market of third-party add-ons or plug-ins that have been designed to assist users in their interactions with ChatGPT and other AI chatbots.

Without delving into specific product reviews, it is important to note that the quality and effectiveness of these tools can vary significantly. Some add-ons make grandiose promises that seem unrealistic, such as the ability to generate a full-length article from just a single keyword. Such promises may lead to disappointment as the outcomes often fall short of expectations.

Others appear to add unnecessary complexity to otherwise straightforward tasks. For example, some plug-ins claim to facilitate the process of crafting a cover letter when users could simply ask the chatbot to create one by supplying their CV and job description. These intermediary tools sometimes operate by obscuring the actual prompts, which can hinder users from learning how to interact directly with the AI system.

There is a concern that relying too heavily on these intermediary tools may detract from the process of developing personal skills and forming a direct understanding of how to work with AI-powered tools. Critical thinking and original ideas remain paramount, both in content production and in the crafting of effective prompts. There is no substitute for these essential human abilities.

That said, it would be remiss not to acknowledge that some third-party plug-ins do provide valuable functionalities that overcome existing limitations in AI-powered chatbots. For example, certain add-ons enable ChatGPT to access the internet or larger files. Others assist in tasks like data analysis or accessing resources like Google Scholar. These tools can add value and enhance the user's experience with the AI systems.

The market for third-party add-ons is evolving at an incredible pace, making it challenging to predict what new functionalities may emerge soon. As this field continues to expand, it will be important for users to approach these tools with discernment, recognizing both the potential benefits and pitfalls. Emphasizing direct engagement, critical assessment, and ongoing learning will likely yield the most rewarding and effective experiences in working with AI chatbots.

Navigating the Conversation

OpenAI's ChatGPT as well as Claude operates within the framework of "conversations" (also called "chats," interchangeably). So, what exactly are these conversations and how can one make the best use of them?

One intriguing characteristic of AI is its capacity for self-awareness, to a certain extent. This means that you can ask the AI directly about its functionalities when you are unsure. I frequently employ this method to enhance my understanding, just as I did to learn about "conversations." Let me share what Chat-GPT provided as a response when I queried about the concept of conversations:

> As an AI language model, my responses are generated based on the entire context of the conversation, not just the early parts. I use natural language processing and machine learning algorithms to analyze and understand the content of the conversation as it progresses, taking into account all the inputs and responses that have been exchanged so far. This allows me to generate responses that are contextually appropriate and relevant to the current stage of the conversation.
>
> In other words, I do not specifically use inputs from the early part of a conversation to produce output for the later parts of the conversation. Instead, I use all the inputs and outputs from the entire conversation to generate responses that are appropriate for the current context. This approach allows me to generate responses that are coherent and relevant to the ongoing conversation, and to adapt to changes in the conversation as they occur.[5]

Similarly, if you attempt to reupload a document to Claude within the same chat, it will tell you that it can see the entire conversation and you do not need to upload it again.

In practical terms, it is advisable to keep separate projects or series of similar requests contained within their own unique conversations. This approach aids AI in contextual comprehension and enables it to carry over stylistic conventions set early in the conversation. For example, keep one conversation open for your emails and memos, another one for grant applications, and yet another for recommendation letters. The efficacy of AI often hinges on the length and depth of the conversation at hand. In essence, the more expansive the conversation, the more AI can grasp the context and nuances of your requests. Consider, for instance, a task as complex and creative as writing a book. It is highly beneficial to contain all related discussions, ideas, and drafts within one sustained conversation with the AI. If you find yourself content with the writing style and the output's quality, maintaining the same conversation for a particular project can be useful, because it saves significant time on rewriting prompts.

Essentially, think of conversations as context depositories. Once you have crafted your first rich prompt, there is no need to duplicate its depth with every subsequent prompt. You can simply instruct the AI to "apply the same style to this fragment," and it will recall your previous prompts. The AI will preserve the style, the overall project's context, and the terminology usage that you have previously established. It increases the value of your best prompts and makes them serve you longer.

During a conversation, you can leverage simpler instructions such as "elucidate," "elaborate," or "restate." However, it is essential to remember that you should consistently provide the AI with portions of text to work with. In fact, after a few very similar prompts like "Elucidate," the chatbot will assume that the next prompt is the same, so you can slide into a promptless request. This approach saves much time if you need to complete many repeated tasks. What I wrote in the section about the rich prompt applies to an entire conversation, not necessarily to every interaction with the conversation.

However, there might come an occasion when the AI appears to wrestle with a form of disarray. This typically surfaces during protracted conversations, particularly when you are incessantly tweaking sections of the same text. The AI may perceive your guidelines as too conflicting, leading to a state that we humanly interpret as "confusion." From the AI's perspective, however, it is more akin to a juggling act of incompatible instructions.

In the process of using AI, you continually revise the same text, each time issuing new, and potentially conflicting, instructions. The AI is programmed to interpret your prompts and react appropriately, all the while retaining knowledge of previous interactions within the conversation. However, when your instructions shift drastically or are contradictory, the AI may have difficulty in determining a coherent course of action.

In these situations, the most prudent course of action may be to relinquish the current conversation and initiate a brand-new one. A fresh conversation functions as a clean slate, devoid of the contradictory elements that clouded the previous discourse. However, it is essential to keep in mind that, within a new conversation, you should reconstruct the elements of a rich prompt. Anytime a chatbot stops making sense, try a new conversation first. If it still does not make sense, the problem is with your prompts.

While AI technology, at this point, is not capable of being tailored precisely to your individual preferences and cannot yet learn your individual writing style and voice, a continuous and expansive conversation is the nearest approximation to such personalization. The AI learns and adjusts based on the cumulative inputs received within the context of the conversation, which can yield results that are surprisingly attuned to your unique needs.

However, for standalone inquiries or tasks, it might be beneficial to delete the conversation once it has served its purpose, so as not to clutter your workspace. This ensures that your interface remains clean and navigable, enhancing your efficiency and productivity.

You will learn to keep some good conversations going for a long time, while others are not worth keeping around.

Stylistic Nuance

When defining the desired writing style, we face a dilemma. Without clear instructions, the output can be generic, clichéd, and lacking individuality. While this may suffice in certain contexts, such as generic business writing, where conformity to conventions is more important than personal expression, it falls short in many other instances. Remember that the language model is trained to recall the most likely combination of words. Therefore, cliché and commonplace expressions are its trademark. On the other hand, if we provide the AI with excessive style directions, we risk creating writing that appears forced and ridiculous. It is a fine line to tread.

Looking ahead, the prospect of training an AI to mimic our personal writing style is undeniably enticing. However, the current limitations on input data size pose an obstacle.

Replicating a personal writing style using AI involves several approaches, each with varying degrees of success. One approach is to use a sample of personal writing as a style guide, feeding it into the AI along with unrelated content, with the expectation that the AI will borrow stylistic elements while disregarding the actual content of the guide. This method can fall short as the AI might integrate actual content from the guide text, undermining the goal of content-independent style replication.

Another strategy involves initially presenting the AI with a piece of personal writing and instructing it to both read and describe the writing style contained within. Using the AI-generated description of the style as a blueprint for subsequent pieces can be more effective. However, this approach might still struggle to capture the distinctive "voice" that characterizes individual writing. It may lack the depth and intricacies that arise from direct perception, leading to an output that pales in comparison to the original.

ChatGPT has recently been employing the so-called "customized instructions," allowing users to store a general description of their preferences for output style. This is a positive development and a step in the right direction. Hopefully, advancements in this direction will continue, leading to more refined and personalized interactions with the AI.

A more effective approach might involve identifying a body of text closely aligned with the desired stylistic preferences and instructing the AI to mirror that style. Directing the AI to emulate the style of essays from renowned publications or drawing inspiration from prolific writers can yield better results. However, even this method reveals the complexity of truly replicating an individual's unique writing style, demonstrating that there are still limitations and challenges in the field of AI-generated content.

It is crucial to exercise caution with this approach. If you instruct the AI to write like specific authors such as David Remnick or Ernest Hemingway, the output may resemble a parody, uncannily close but somehow missing the mark. Instead, it might be more advisable to select a broader corpus of works from several authors whose writing styles you admire. For example, consider giving an instruction like this: "Make it sound like a typical *The New Yorker* non-fiction essay."

This strategy brings up an interesting ethical question about the emulation of someone else's writing style. Is this not something we do during our education?

Do we not read books and learn how to write from others? Have not many great writers acknowledged their debt to others they learned from?

By studying and incorporating the collective influences of multiple authors who share similarities with your preferred style, you can avoid the pitfalls of imitating a single author too closely. This method leverages the breadth of their work to develop distinctive AI-generated output that genuinely reflects your voice, striking a balance between drawing inspiration and maintaining authenticity.

Another trick is to start each segment you wish to edit with a well-written paragraph in your preferred style. Include in your prompt an instruction like this: "Use the first paragraph as the guiding style sample."

However, this approach is not without its challenges. Manual editing may be necessary to refine elements that fall short of an authentic personal voice. In fact, one of the advanced skills at which humans so far outperform the AI is the ability to tweak style, to create a unique voice.

There is a threshold beyond which crafting the piece personally becomes more efficient. The decision hinges on the significance you attribute to your individual voice for the specific writing endeavor. Perhaps voice is less important in an accreditation report, so you can ignore the style altogether ю

Although AI can save significant time on text generation, expect to spend a bit more time on editing. The overall time savings are still very impressive but do allocate enough time for re-reading and editing the final product. We will return to this important point in the section on authorship. The authorial responsibility is shifting from the act of text generation to the act of the release of the text to the world.

In this captivating exploration of personalizing AI writing, we balance efficiency and authenticity. As we move closer to a future where AI can faithfully reflect our individual writing styles, the inherent, irreplaceable value of the human touch in writing must be acknowledged. Despite AI's remarkable advancements, the idiosyncratic beauty of human expression remains an art form of its own, illustrating that some nuances of personal style may forever lie beyond the reach of even the most advanced computers.

How Does It Feel?

The experience of writing with AI, or what I like to call "wraiting," is an adventure into uncharted territories, a type of experience that may initially feel unfamiliar and challenging. Ironically, the better a writer you are, the more confusing AI assistance may initially feel. Nevertheless, this undertaking is not as daunting as rocket science, and it is important to approach it with an open mind, curiosity, and a sense of adventure. This section is my attempt to prepare you psychologically for learning how to "wraite."

Once upon a time, writing was a solitary endeavor. But with AI's involvement, it has transformed into a creative partnership, where you are not the only participant. Although some might perceive this change as dystopian, I view it as an era of "wraiting"—a harmonious blend of traditional writing and AI, forming an intriguing symbiotic relationship. Only very few people who have experience working with ghostwriters and speechwriters have something in their experience to prepare them for this shift.

"Wraiting" requires one to set aside any anxieties about the content generated. One needs to overcome the traditional demarcation between "mine" and "not mine." When text is crafted from your AI-guided prompts, even if it does not mirror your usual style or voice, it is vital to perceive it as yours. Or, rather, what is important and original there is yours, and whatever is not yours is common knowledge. Consider this as interacting with an alternate version of yourself, a digital reflection contributing to your creative process. This way, you can fully embrace the potential of writing and let this new form of expression enhance your creativity.

The first time you try "wraiting" with a chatbot, it can feel weird. When the chatbot quickly produces a well-written piece, you might think, "Wow! I have spent years learning how to write well, and this machine can do something similar in no time!" It is surprising and a little unsettling to see a machine do something you have worked hard to be good at.

This unsettling feeling is not unique to our tech-infused era, nor is it exclusive to the white-collar demographic. Let us turn the clock back to the 18th and 19th centuries, during the heyday of the Industrial Revolution. Craftsmen, renowned for their skills and the impeccable quality of their handiwork, found their lives upended by the advent of mass production.

The birth of factories manufacturing goods at a fraction of the price of artisanal products posed an existential threat to these craftsmen. Consider the humble shoemaker who crafted footwear with painstaking precision, suddenly confronted by an avalanche of shoes churned out by mechanical marvels at prices his handcrafted shoes could not compete with. This shift exerted immense economic pressure, compelling craftsmen to either adapt their skills to the new industrial world order or seek alternate professions. We do not have to travel too far back; several occupations have shrunk or disappeared during our lifetimes: travel agents, video store clerks, photo film developers, map printers, phone book publishers, and bank tellers. How do you think all these people felt? Naturally, their initial reaction was one of disbelief and outright denial.

Yet, as I navigated through my initial wave of discomfort with AI, I noticed its limitations and constraints. And I will confess that this revelation brought with it a sigh of relief. Recognizing AI's weaknesses made me realize that I possess something that it does not. Thus, the initial and perhaps the most crucial step is to maintain a calm and collected demeanor in the face of AI. Staying composed enables further learning. It means avoiding panic and not dismissing AI as a trivial gimmick. Navigating between the extremes of fear and denial allows you to weather this period of transition and progress further into the intriguing world of "wraiting."

The novelty of AI tools tends to fade as you become more familiar with their use. With about a month's worth of daily practical use, these tools become less of a wonder and more of an everyday utility. You start understanding their capabilities and limitations more deeply, and the output they generate becomes increasingly predictable. The initial sense of magic gradually dissipates, reinforcing the fact that, at its core, an AI is ultimately just a cleverly designed instrument.

As I ventured deeper into the world of "wraiting," I began to acknowledge that crafting sentences, while a cornerstone of writing, could sometimes be a laborious task worthy of being outsourced. This realization comes easier with professional communications such as reports, applications, recommendations, and letters, where personal voice often takes a backseat to the conventional structure and format. As I entrusted these tasks to AI, my frustrations over maintaining voice and authorship receded, providing the cognitive schemata to differentiate between those aspects of writing that can be delegated to AI and those that demand human mind.

Interestingly, using AI to handle some of the basic writing tasks did not make me care less about the quality; it made me focus on it more. By letting the AI do some of the initial work, I had more energy to look closely at the details of the text. I spent more time than before considering word choices, sentence structure, and style. This did not show a problem with the AI, but rather gave me something valuable: more time. The time I used to spend on the basic writing tasks could now be used for careful editing. In this way, using "wraiting" saved me time on the initial steps, allowing me to put more effort into improving the final product.

Yet, it is important to note that my journey and the epiphanies along the way are not universal blueprints. They signify a personal choice, a distinctive trail I have elected to traverse. Not everyone may find the same delight or sense of creative emancipation through "wraiting." But its potential is undeniable—"wraiting" can redefine our relationship with the written word, economizing our efforts on foundational tasks and enabling us to ascend toward more advanced creative heights.

AI, always polite and calm, can be likened to a personal assistant. The assistant may not be the brightest you ever had, but it is incredibly fast, is very well informed in all disciplines and fields, does not get annoyed or tired, and does not ask for a paycheck. Where humans get tired of repetitive tasks, AI only learns more. It is always ready to perform tasks that I would rather not do myself. The overall experience is more liberatory than confining.

The Art of Chunking

One critical aspect to be cognizant of is understanding the optimal text size for interactions with AI chatbots. Knowing the size limitations of text that these AI models can handle is crucial to obtaining high-quality outputs and ensuring efficient interaction. I hope this is a temporary condition, but it is also likely that scarcity of processing capacity will present an ongoing natural limit to expanding the text size capacity. The input and output sizes are two very different things.

If you have tried to feed in a text longer than ChatGPT's comfort zone, which is approximately 2000 words, you would likely receive a response indicating that the text is too long. As users, we need to be mindful of these constraints to avoid input overload and to ensure that our AI companion works in its most effective range. Starting with October 2023, ChatGPT allows limited file uploads. Claude, however, will accept very large texts, in various file formats, up to 5 files, 10 Mb each. It is coy about disclosing the exact word count limitation, but it can take 50,000 words in plain text for a high-level analysis. It will not edit, or revise the entire text, but can provide a critique or write a review, an outline, or suggest improvements.

Generally, both ChatGPT and Claude tend to produce outputs of about 500–600 words. With some prodding, Claude can generate a 1500-word text, but it may be diminished in quality. You might ask, "Is this a hard limit?" The answer is no; it is not a rigid restriction. Instead, think of it as a rule of thumb or a guide that helps you better utilize ChatGPT or Claude. When we provide our AI tools with information within their optimal processing range, we are more likely to get outputs that are both accurate and useful.

Imagine you have a comprehensive report or a lengthy essay of about 6000 words that you want ChatGPT to process. To handle this efficiently, you would need to divide the document into smaller chunks because the optimal output lies somewhere in the ballpark of 600 words. This means you should think about breaking it down into approximately 10 chunks in terms of output. If you use the technique of "sloppy jotting" that I describe later in the book, you will have to produce inputs that will be OK after growing to about 500–600 words.

At first glance, this might seem like an extra step. However, consider this: Working in smaller chunks compels you to think about the structure of your content more consciously. You are encouraged to divide your text into manageable parts that are easier for the chatbot not only to handle but also to streamline the review and editing process. The result is an efficient workflow that maintains high standards of output quality.

Often, we might feel the urge to provide as much information as possible to the AI, believing that more data will yield better results. However, the size limitation necessitates a different approach. It encourages us to be more selective, to remove redundant or peripheral information, and to focus on presenting the core content. This distillation of input can have a remarkable effect on the output, enhancing its relevance, precision, and overall quality.

In essence, these constraints act as a helpful filter. They push us to focus on delivering a concise and relevant input, which allows the chatbot to generate a more targeted and accurate output. This disciplined approach to interacting with AI can significantly improve the effectiveness of the AI models we work with, leading to better results in our tasks and projects.

Approach a longer text in stages. Start by writing down your ideas; there should be enough of them for a scholarly paper. Nothing can replace this initial step, although, as I will show, AI can be used for brainstorming and preliminary research. Then ask the AI to turn your rough ideas into an outline, and complete with summaries for each proposed subheading. The AI's unique capability of understanding the progression of a linear argument comes into play here, helping you to streamline and consolidate your thoughts. You will find that similar ideas that you might have considered as separate entities are gathered under one subheading, enhancing the clarity and coherence of your outline.

This strategic chunking ensures that your resulting content is well-paced. It prevents your narrative from feeling rushed or, conversely, from becoming too diluted. It ensures that your output maintains a balanced level of detail and flow, which is key to creating engaging, readable content.

This technique not only optimizes the AI's text-processing capabilities but also supports you in constructing a well-structured, coherent narrative. In essence, this approach is a practical hack to navigate the size constraints of AI models and to leverage their capabilities for generating longer texts more efficiently.

As previously discussed, there have been numerous attempts to expand both input and output sizes. Claude provides a direct method for inputting larger files, while ChatGPT can accommodate this through third-party plug-ins. However, overcoming the constraints on output size appears to be more challenging. Even if techniques are employed to coax the AI into producing a more expansive text, the quality seems to decline rapidly with the increase in size. It is likely that the necessity for dividing the content into manageable sections, or "chunking," will remain a consideration for the foreseeable future.

Notes

1 Shakked Noy and Whitney Zhang, "Experimental Evidence on the Productivity Effects of Generative Artificial Intelligence," available at SSRN 4375283 (2023), https://www.science.org/doi/10.1126/science.adh2586
2 Everett M. Rogers, *Diffusion of Innovations* (New York: The Free Press of Glencoe, 1962).
3 Alexander M. Sidorkin, "Tool Fetishism in Online Teaching," 2020, https://sidorkin.blogspot.com/2020/08/tool-fetishism-in-online-teaching.html
4 Kyle Wiggers, "Anthropic Releases Claude 2, Its Second-gen AI Chatbot," *Techcrunch*, July 11, 2023, https://techcrunch.com/2023/07/11/anthropic-releases-claude-2-the-second-generation-of-its-ai-chatbot/
5 OpenAI's GPT-4. Chat, 7/22/2023.

2 Instruction

In this chapter, we explore the use of AI in teaching with two main aims: improving the teaching process for educators and reshaping the skills taught to students. These objectives, while overlapping in many areas, have unique elements that justify distinct focus.

Our first aim is to equip faculty with AI tools to simplify and elevate their teaching. Most higher education faculty members have not received formal teaching instruction, often learning the craft through personal experience, guidance from senior colleagues, or university-provided resources. AI can serve as a personal instructional designer, aiding without judgment and offering insights tailored to your discipline. In my view, refusing its aid is a missed opportunity.

Even for accomplished instructors, AI's application can alleviate burdens such as grading test development and designing evaluation rubrics, while allowing educators to concentrate on dynamic and imaginative teaching methods. AI can offer personalized insights into each student's learning style and progress, leading to more precise and effective teaching strategies. Furthermore, AI can assist in creating stimulating learning materials, from interactive digital content to AI-augmented lesson plans, thereby enriching the overall educational experience.

The second objective underscores the need to reconsider the skills we instill in students considering rapid technological advancements. Traditional skills may no longer suffice in a world where AI is poised to take over routine tasks. As such, it is crucial to shift the focus toward skills that will remain uniquely human, such as critical thinking, creativity, empathy, and the ability to work with AI. This also necessitates eliminating or reducing emphasis on certain skills that are likely to become obsolete due to automation. A recent LinkedIn report says that 45% of teaching can be automated with AI, allowing instructors to spend more time on other aspects of their job.[1] Those are "Lesson Planning, Curriculum Development, Teacher Training, Literacy, and Tutoring."

While these two objectives are connected in various ways, they also stand apart. For instance, one might advocate for the use of AI to enhance teaching efficiencies without necessarily agreeing with a revamp of the educational curriculum based on future AI projections.

DOI: 10.4324/9781032686028-2

However, I strongly believe in both imperatives. As educators, we must take a proactive approach to equip our students with the right tools and skills to navigate this changing landscape. And we owe it to ourselves to make our teaching less time-consuming and more effective.

Stop the Panic, Embrace the Future

My concerns lie heavily with the potential mismanagement of the AI revolution by the higher education community, should we insist on adhering to our time-honored practices and conventions. I have already heard many professors argue that the exclusive approach to teaching writing should be the enforcement of conventional pedagogy. These individuals mirror their predecessors who, not too long ago, staunchly advocated that the only correct method of mastering handwriting was to wield the traditional quill pen and shy away from innovations such as fountain pens.

I am primarily concerned with the proliferation of prohibitive policies, where faculty require students to sign an oath not to use ChatGPT in their class assignments. Another manifestation of the same sentiment is the attempt to develop software that would detect the use of AI in a text. This approach is misguided and makes our profession look weak and backward rather than strong and forward-looking. Prohibitive policies are hard to defend because they are based on false premises. Enforcing a policy that is difficult to defend is unethical; it is an exercise of raw power over students without being able to provide a rationale.

Take the often-heard objection: "You cannot use ChatGPT because you have to learn to write on your own." The underlying premise here is that people will not be using AI in their jobs and civic life. However, this is clearly not true. We see the explosive growth in the use of AI in all areas of life, and this trend shows no signs of slowing down. In fact, it is too much of a gain in productivity to go away. Therefore, we must prepare students for a lifetime of using AI.

Remember how we burdened school children with memorizing multiplication tables, anticipating that hypothetical moment on a deserted island with no calculator at hand? Now every cell phone has a calculator, and every person has a cell phone. It is entirely possible to be successful in the contemporary world without knowing multiplication tables. So, we have wasted countless hours teaching children a now-obsolete skill while not teaching them the skills they need. Should we not at least try to avoid making the same mistake with writing?

A second version of the argument against classroom AI goes like this: "You have to learn the mechanics of writing because, without understanding the fundamentals, you will not be able to generate or edit appropriate text, even with AI." This objection assumes a linear curriculum, suggesting that mastering the basics must precede acquiring more complex skills like original thinking or discernment. Advocates of traditional writing pedagogy propose a certain sequence: master the mechanics of writing first before tackling the more complex and advanced skills associated with "wraiting." Yet, the correlation between writing mechanics and higher-order skills like original and discerning thinking is not necessarily linear.

This debate over the merits of a linear or sequential curriculum has been longstanding among theorists, but I will not delve into a full review here. The empirical evidence backing this approach is, at best, inconsistent. Despite the conviction of many educators that a linear curriculum is essential for teaching complex skills such as writing, these beliefs lack robust empirical support. To date, there has not been a high-quality meta-analysis that conclusively demonstrates the efficacy of a linear curriculum. On the other hand, alternative teaching methodologies like problem-based learning, which are inherently non-linear, have shown significant positive impacts on student learning.[2]

Furthermore, anecdotal evidence often points in the opposite direction. Learning can be a non-linear, exploratory process. One might first acquire a sophisticated skill and then proceed to fill in the gaps by studying the more basic mechanical aspects of a discipline, a sort of reverse engineering of knowledge. Not every exceptional editor is necessarily an exceptional writer; these are two distinct skills. Similarly, not every accomplished conductor is a composer, and not every theater critic is a playwright.

Students could initially learn the advanced skill of "wraiting" by leveraging AI to generate a meaningful, complex text. Through this, they will also understand the mechanics of writing, gaining some insight into what happens "under the hood" of their AI-assisted compositions. Could they be at a disadvantage later in life, struggling to craft a decent sentence on their own?

My final argument against prohibiting AI in the classroom is this: I use AI-powered writing tools every day, many times a day, as do many others in academia. You, the reader, will do the same if you are not doing it already. Given this trajectory, what moral or pedagogical ground do we have to prevent students from learning to use a tool that is increasingly indispensable? Institutions that opt for a no-AI policy now might soon find themselves scrambling to revise their guidelines, confronted by technology's pervasive role in daily life. Now is a short window of time to avoid future embarrassment.

What requires serious consideration is the significant disservice we might inflict on our students if we neglect to foresee the impending transformations in the professional spheres, civic, and cultural life for which we are equipping them. Holding onto traditional writing instruction is irresponsible, considering it will soon be supplanted by the practice of "wraiting." This shift is already occurring rapidly. Insisting on imparting yesterday's skills contradicts our duty toward the student body, if indeed their welfare is our priority.

The inevitable incursion of AI into various domains of our existence elicits a mixed reaction of wonder, doubt, and trepidation. Its foray into the educational sphere, particularly in writing, has sparked apprehension that the upcoming generation may not learn to write independently. This fear escalates into a more formidable prospect as some prognosticate a substantial degradation of a fundamental human ability, culminating in cultural impoverishment.

Nevertheless, I find myself detached from these apprehensions. I envision a metamorphosis of skills rather than their annihilation. It becomes apparent that the professional landscape is in perpetual motion, and our educational infrastructures must possess the flexibility to adjust correspondingly.

It is conceivable that the capability to craft grammatically sound sentences may become as obsolete as penmanship. The focus would likely shift to skills inherently dependent on human capacity, such as creativity, idea generation, and the ability to create an input for, and then evaluate and select, a lucid and expressive text. I realize this is a difficult fact to accept, but I urge the reader to consider it. Imagine a world where the ability to string a sentence together is no longer impressive. Ideas and discernment, not eloquence, will be valued and rewarded. Despite the change in tools, the foundational principles of communication—clarity and engagement—would maintain their prominence. Essentially, everyone is being promoted from a writer to an editor, which on balance seems beneficial.

It is highly probable that, as technology advances, people will utilize the capabilities of AI in innovative ways, some of which are beyond our current imagination. For instance, if you are a counselor, you might soon be able to record each session with a client and receive an in-depth content analysis of the client's speech. This could reveal insights or patterns you may have initially missed. Or consider being a classroom teacher equipped with AI that can provide immediate feedback on your teaching methods, drawn from an analysis of audio or video recordings from your lessons.

If you are a nurse, AI could serve as a second pair of eyes, meticulously reviewing doctors' notes to catch potential errors or omissions. Likewise, communication specialists could leverage AI to draft multiple versions of a message tailored for different audiences and platforms, along with predictions on how engaging each version is likely to be.

In a future like this, the skills that will be in high demand will not revolve around minor grammatical choices, such as whether to use a colon or a semicolon. Instead, the focus will shift toward the ability to design and manage workflows that are significantly enhanced by AI assistance.

It is crucial to relinquish the assumption that the world our students will enter will be identical to ours. We must prepare them for a future where AI is integrated into many aspects of professional and personal life, which includes understanding how to effectively utilize AI in their writing. After considerable thought and external inquiry, I find no reason, short of a global catastrophe, why people would cease using AI for generating text and other content. This is not a distant, hypothetical scenario, but a reality rapidly taking shape. It is high time we acknowledged this impending change and adjusted our educational strategies accordingly.

Far from impoverishing our culture, the emergence of "wraiting" could potentially enrich it. Just as the advent of digital technology has expanded our ability to create and share content, the integration of AI into the writing process could introduce new forms of expression and communication. It could democratize writing by making it more accessible, allow us to generate content more efficiently, and open new avenues for creativity.

The consequences of this transition remain uncertain. This future scenario may or may not result in a reduced workforce; that is still unclear. Even so, resisting productivity gains for the sake of retaining more jobs embodies the Luddite fallacy, which has proven detrimental to societies that have embraced it.

We can debate the potential impact of this shift on people's happiness. In my view, it is likely to enhance job satisfaction by freeing individuals from the tedium of routine tasks, allowing them to focus more on the creative and strategic aspects of their work. Even if you disagree with this perspective, the likelihood of this change is hard to deny.

Original and Discerning Thinking

In this section, I will discuss the need for a pedagogical shift toward teaching original and discerning thinking, and away from writing mechanics.

Original thinking and related concepts of creative and divergent thinking have been explored for a long time.[3] By discerning thinking, I mean a cognitive process characterized by nuanced understanding, judgment, and evaluation of content such as text generated by AI. It is the ability to choose well. This process goes beyond simple good vs. bad judgment, demanding the extraction of intricate details, nuances, and implications from the given information, ideas, or alternatives. To effectively practice discerning thinking, individuals must be able to distinguish between valid and invalid arguments, bad and good writing, identify biases and likely falsehoods, and comprehend the consequences of differing versions of the same content.

In contexts marked by multiple viable options, perspectives, or solutions, discernment as a skill becomes vital. It enables individuals to carefully assess each alternative to make the most informed and advantageous decision. This form of thinking, underpinned by keen attention to detail, the ability to identify inconsistencies, and a deep understanding of the relevant context, is essential in professions that necessitate complex problem-solving or decision-making in uncertain environments, such as management, law, medicine, and academia.

My principal assertion is that we must adjust our pedagogy to shift the focus from the fundamentals of writing to original and discerning thinking, using AI-powered tools to accomplish this transition. This strategy is a better alternative to panicking about plagiarism and attempting to preserve the unsavable—the traditional writing assignment.

In the landscape of education, AI, and its role in the process of writing—or rather "wraiting"—is viewed with no small measure of trepidation. Critics, often educators themselves, opine that students relying on AI chatbots for composition are at risk of never learning to write on their own, to craft prose in their own voice. This argument hinges on an age-old assumption, one that views traditional writing as an essential skill that will forever be in demand. As we discussed in the previous section, that is simply not true.

Setting the argument about the linearity of learning aside, there is a more general question. Can AI truly serve as a catalyst for cognitive growth? And if so, how?

"Wraiting" is not less sophisticated or satisfying than traditional writing. These two skills are overlapping, sharing significant commonalities, but their focal points and emphases diverge. If anything, "wraiting" could be considered more fundamentally human, as it amplifies the role of distinctly human capabilities, while relinquishing those tasks that can be automated. The mechanics of writing are truly machine-like and should be delegated to machines.

We first need to understand that AI, in this context, goes beyond being a mere tool for efficiency or automation. Rather, we position AI as an interactive agent capable of stimulating cognitive growth in learners. It is through engaging with AI, understanding its workings, and even predicting its output that students can sharpen their advanced cognitive skills.

Let us compare the subsets of skills associated with traditional writing and "wraiting":

Traditional Writing: grammar, spelling, punctuation, vocabulary, organization, structure, coherence, clarity, conciseness, style, tone, research, editing, revising, creativity, originality, thesis development, citation management.

"Wraiting": original thinking, discerning thinking, prompt development and tuning, output evaluation, mastery of styles and genres, collaboration, adaptability, taste, intuition, text structuring, contextual knowledge for assessing veracity, advanced search skills.

Upon closer examination, it becomes apparent that "wraiting" requires a more advanced skill set compared to traditional writing. In essence, teaching the use of AI for text production does not represent a step down in cognitive complexity; rather, it is a step up. It challenges learners to develop and utilize advanced cognitive skills to effectively collaborate with AI, elevating their overall writing and thinking abilities in the process. This is a trade-up, not a trade-down. We move to raise expectations, not to lower them.

When we generate ideas, we often do so in a raw and unfiltered form. Our thoughts are jumbled and disconnected, and it can be difficult to articulate them in a way that others can understand. Writing requires us to take these raw ideas and refine them into a more coherent and structured form. This process often involves editing and revision, as we work to clarify and simplify our ideas for our intended audience.

AI algorithms are designed to analyze and restructure text in a way that is more easily understood by others. This often involves simplifying complex ideas and concepts, removing jargon or technical language, and rearranging sentence structures to make them more readable. Innocently, it will cut out your best ideas for that exact reason.

However, it is important to note that AI is not always successful in this task. While AI can be helpful in generating and refining written content, it can also be limited by its programming and training data. AI models are only as good as the data they are trained on, and they may struggle to understand or convey certain ideas that are outside the scope of their programming. To foster thinking, students need to be taught to understand these limitations. Understanding the limitations of an instrument is also a cognitively sophisticated skill transferrable to other domains.

As the final note of this section, I will offer a hypothesis. Not only professors, but many other professionals, often discount unfamiliar knowledge, while valuing the knowledge they already possess. It is understandable; one needs to sell one's expertise in the marketplace. This is why there is so much anxiety about AI among professors. It is about us, not about our students. We should not allow this common bias of self-importance to overshadow the clear and significant advantages of teaching students how to harness AI for enhancing their work and life skills. Just because we do not yet fully understand how to teach this does not render the skill any less relevant or crucial. It is our responsibility to investigate and understand this field for the benefit of our students. We are the grown-ups in the room, and telling our students to stay away from the biggest technological breakthrough of this century is not a grown-up thing to do.

Writing Assessments

In this section, we delve into the disruption that AI introduces to the conventional use of written text in assessments. Specifically, we focus on strategies to re-engineer assignments to capitalize on AI capabilities, such as those offered by ChatGPT or Claude, rather than simply dismissing them.

Think about it this way: if an AI can successfully complete a writing assignment that you have designed, that might be a clue that your assignment needs re-assessment and revision. You can perform what I call "the lazy prompt test" quite easily. Just copy your assignment description from the syllabus or a Learning Management System shell, paste it into a chatbot like ChatGPT, and ask it to write the assignment. If the bot produces a satisfactory result, it is an indicator that your assignment or at least its evaluation rubric may need a rethink.

I want to make it abundantly clear: if you add even just a few key ideas or examples to a generic assignment prompt taken from your syllabus, it transforms into what I call a "rich prompt." *Any* assignment can be aced in this manner, and that is precisely what we want students to learn—how to generate and communicate their original thoughts. With the addition of original ideas, an AI-generated text ceases to be fraudulent and becomes an artifact of authentic authorship.

There is a significant pragmatic and ethical difference between "lazy" and "rich" prompts, and between using AI without original thought and AI supplemented with original work.

Rather than resisting the rise of AI by discouraging students from using it, it is perhaps more practical to acknowledge and adapt to this change by rethinking your assignments. The advent of AI in educational settings necessitates a thorough reevaluation of our basic educational methodologies. It forces us to question the efficacy and relevance of traditional forms of writing assessments, especially when an AI can convincingly replicate the output of an average student. While this scenario does not offer easy solutions, it does provide a unique opportunity to reshape our understanding of writing and its role in cultivating critical thinking.

The emergence of AI underscores a significant reality: our traditional educational and assessment methods are no longer infallible. Our focus should shift toward teaching students to think creatively and discern wisely. As AI capabilities grow, our aim should be to enhance our uniquely human qualities. To prevent widespread cheating by students, instructors need to learn to develop a cheat-proof course. It is a course where cheating is either impossible or too time-consuming to make sense.

Traditionally revered, especially in the humanities, social sciences, and professional fields, written assignments serve dual purposes: they are both exercises for skill development and means of assessment. These assignments transcend the mere parroting of facts. Instead, they enable students to demonstrate applied knowledge and articulate their thoughts clearly and compellingly.

In comparison to multiple-choice tests, the advantages of written assignments are manifold. They eliminate the element of guesswork and allow students to exhibit a nuanced grasp of the subject matter. Moreover, they can be engineered to offer iterative feedback, thereby encouraging sustained learning. Yet, these assignments are not without their downsides: they are labor-intensive to evaluate and susceptible to plagiarism—a vulnerability that has become more glaring in our digitally connected age. The advent of AI-powered chatbots has heightened these vulnerabilities to an almost untenable level, pushing traditional written assignments to a crisis point.

The spectrum of written assignments is vast, spanning from research papers to argumentative essays, from literary analyses to personal narratives. Beyond these, think about specialized written tasks such as case reports, lesson plans, project proposals, analytical reports, evaluations, and treatment plans. Each of these demands rigorous planning, extensive research, and meticulous revision. They also require students to master the art of written language, from grammar to stylistic conventions. In essence, written assignments are cornerstone tools in fostering critical thinking and preparing students for the intellectual demands of academia and the professional world.

Given the profound roles that written assignments have traditionally played, it is naive to think we can simply jettison them because AI chatbots have entered the stage. Rather, we should explore strategies that incorporate AI capabilities into the fabric of the assignments themselves. Our aim is to identify viable ways to integrate AI into higher education, particularly in courses where writing is a key component.

We have three options at our disposal:

1. We could revise assignments to require students using AI and evaluate their skills of doing so which is the focus on this section.
2. There is a possibility of a tool-neutral assignment, where students have an option to use AI or not. We will also explore it here.
3. We could replace written assignments with alternative forms of assessment, such as oral exams or multiple-choice tests—a topic I will explore in the next section.

Let us consider option 1. Imagine an assignment centered around honing students' skills in creating "rich prompts" and critically evaluating AI-produced texts. In other words, the assignment would emphasize creative and discerning thinking, but also assess the upskills related to navigating AI-powered tools. In this task, students would engage with an AI language model, such as ChatGPT, to produce a piece of writing pertaining to their course. The assignment would encourage students to refine their prompts iteratively, working toward eliciting a high-quality response from the AI. Following this, they would need to assess the final output, considering the relevant concepts learned in class, absence of errors, the quality of the writing, and the degree to which it encapsulates their original ideas.

To ensure the effective implementation of this assignment, educators would need to demonstrate the process of prompt development in the classroom. They could work through several iterations with the whole class, demonstrating the steps of prompt creation, evaluation, and refinement. Educators would also need to consider the volume and length of the AI-generated text they would receive and assess the time required for its review.

Students would be tasked with choosing a topic relevant to their course for an in-depth examination. They would construct an initial prompt for the AI model, using guidelines for crafting rich prompts. They could leverage any of the sample prompts provided as a starting point, with the goal of enhancing these through subsequent iterations.

Upon receiving the AI-generated output, students would evaluate its quality, relevance, and depth and pinpoint areas for enhancement. Based on this evaluation, they would modify their prompt and elicit a new response from the AI. This iterative process would continue until the students are satisfied with the quality of the AI-generated text.

Once the AI-generated text meets their standards, students could manually edit the final version and submit their sequence of prompts, the AI's last response, and their edited text. There should be a way to compare the written products produced by individual students or teams, with an analysis of the best examples.

The assignment grading would be based on students' ability to generate rich prompts and their capacity to evaluate and edit the AI-produced text. Additional factors include the clarity and originality of their idea, the inclusion of specific examples, the adequacy of the writing, the veracity of claims, and the successful application of concepts learned in class.

Incorporating AI in traditional writing assignments represents a profound shift, signifying the beginning of a journey that could redefine how we teach and assess our students. As AI continues to advance, it is up to us to adapt and to integrate these tools into our classrooms in meaningful and productive ways. I imagine it would take thousands of experiments to get the AI-focused writing assignment right across many disciplines.

To make the AI-assisted writing assignment work, consider pushing it as close as possible to the direction of authentic assessment. In the realm of curriculum theory, we come across the notion of "authentic assessment." This evaluation methodology involves applying the skills and knowledge that have been learned to real-world scenarios or tasks pertinent to the subject of study. Rather than merely testing isolated skills or rote memorized facts, authentic assessment necessitates that students demonstrate understanding and competence through tasks that align closely with the practical application of those skills outside the academic environment. For instance, instead of penning a theoretical "teaching philosophy," future educators might draft genuine cover letters for job applications. Psychology students, rather than writing research papers solely for the instructor, may submit an actual paper to a scholarly journal. Computer science students, instead of writing code for an abstract scenario, may seek out real-world projects on and off campus in need of their expertise. When it comes to a writing assignment that necessitates the use of AI, the more the project aligns with authentic assessment, the more valuable and meaningful it will prove to be. In fact, the use of AI will make student projects closer to the products expected in the real world.

To create authentic AI-centered writing assignments, we must have an idea how students will be using such skills in the real world. This may not be easy, because most of the professions have not figured it out yet.

This form of education nurtures a discerning perspective, empowering students to make sophisticated judgments about nuances within seemingly similar outputs. The ability to distinguish subtle differences and understand the implications of various choices within the text is of utmost importance. This sort of discernment is not solely a matter of identifying what has been generated by the AI, but also a deeper analysis of why certain parts work better, why some arguments are more compelling, or why some word choices create a more potent impact. This critical engagement with the AI-produced text forms an integral part of the learning process, fostering original thinking and discerning judgment in students.

The second option on the table is for instructors to adopt a stance of deliberate indifference toward students' use of AI, grading them solely on the quality of the product. While I find this approach inferior to explicitly guiding students in harnessing the power of AI, it has its own litmus test: task ChatGPT or Claude with grading a real student paper using your existing rubric. You might be shocked to find that the AI's grading prowess is remarkably accurate, often mirroring the grade you would have given.

Now, here is the kicker: re-grade that same paper using a rubric that factors in the elements that truly matter in authentic intellectual work. Think originality, a distinct voice, eloquence, and contextual appropriateness—benchmarked against the best written work in your field. In my case, that is the Philosophy of Education Yearbook. You may find that the paper that easily snagged an "A" under your traditional criteria is now in a failing territory.

By leveraging writing tools, we are not dumbing down expectations; we are ratcheting them up. Ditch the paternalistic "good enough for undergrads" mindset. Elevate the bar, prioritizing advanced skills over the mechanical aspects of writing. And for the love of all that is intellectual, stop obsessing over APA or MLA formats. That is precisely the kind of drudgery AI can handle, liberating human cognition for higher-order tasks.

In sum, if you flirt with this second option, you will likely gravitate toward explicit instruction on AI-assisted writing anyway. Because when we are in the business of pedagogy, why miss an opportunity to make it exceptional? You will also find quickly that students vary widely in their ability to harness the full power of chatbots in academic writing. Instructors should not accept that inequity and try to address it.

Naturally, to effectively assess a student's work with AI, the instructors must first master the skills they aim to impart. This involves not only a comprehension of the technical aspects of AI, but also a keen understanding of the cognitive processes associated with engaging this technology—including original thinking, critical evaluation, and discerning judgment. The instructor's role then becomes less about imparting knowledge and developing basic skills in the traditional sense, and more about coaching students in the effective use of AI as a cognitive tool. It is my sincere hope that this book will inspire educators to acquire these competencies, enabling them to foster these valuable skills in as many students as possible.

Alternative Assessments

To compensate for the demise of traditional writing assessments, the third strategy is to use more of the non-writing performance-based assessments we used before. While writing assignments have long been the cornerstone of academic evaluation, they are by no means the only instrument at our disposal.

A broad palette of assessment strategies exists, each with its own unique merits. Performance-based assessments are a type of academic evaluation that measure students' abilities to apply skills and knowledge in real-world scenarios. I am fully aware that these are not equally applicable across all disciplines. If you teach theoretical physics, envisioning a performance assessment is difficult. If you teach studio art, nothing is more natural. There is a spectrum between where performance assessments are possible, but to varying degrees. In many cases they can replace traditional writing assessments, which, as we have established, may not function optimally in the age of AI.

These assessments often involve tasks or projects that require students to demonstrate their understanding of a concept or idea through practical application. Here are some examples of performance-based academic assessments:

1. Oral presentations and oral exams—In this type of assessment, students are required to present information on a topic or idea verbally in front of their peers or an audience. This can include delivering a speech, a debate, or a group presentation. The assessment focuses on the students' ability to organize their thoughts, communicate clearly and effectively, and engage the audience.
2. Portfolio assessments—These involve compiling a collection of student work, such as essays, lab reports, or other projects, which demonstrates their mastery of a particular skill or concept. The assessment is based on the quality of work and the students' ability to reflect on their own learning and progress. While each individual element of a portfolio may be written with AI's help, the ability to present a comprehensive picture of one's progress is what needs to be evaluated primarily.
3. Simulations and games—Simulations involve creating a real-world scenario in which students must apply their knowledge and skills to achieve a particular goal. This can include computer simulations, role-playing scenarios, or other immersive experiences. The assessment focuses on the students' ability to apply knowledge, make decisions, and demonstrate practical skills.
4. Experiential learning—This involves students engaging in hands-on experiences that allow them to apply their knowledge and skills in a real-world setting. This can include internships, service learning, or apprenticeships. The assessment focuses on the students' ability to apply their knowledge and skills in a real-world setting and reflect on their own learning and growth.

Performance-based assessments offer a far richer snapshot of a student's capabilities than do traditional formats like multiple-choice tests. These assessments allow students to demonstrate their mastery of skills and knowledge in a real-world setting, preparing them for success in their future careers.

These influences could undermine performance-based assessments in some ways, while strengthening them in others. For oral presentations, while AI speech recognition technology can aid in transcription, it cannot evaluate factors like body language, tone, or audience engagement, preserving the need for human assessment. While AI can streamline digital portfolios and critique writing quality, it falls short in assessing the nuanced qualities of work and personal reflection. Performance tasks, although less vulnerable to AI-aided cheating, still require human evaluators to assess aspects such as creativity and originality. AI can enhance the complexity of simulations and provide certain performance feedback, but human evaluators are still needed for assessing critical thinking and problem-solving skills. For experiential learning, AI can help track measurable factors, but it cannot assess soft skills like communication, teamwork, and leadership. In sum, although AI contributes powerful tools, it neither replaces the necessity for human assessment in performance-based evaluations nor absolves us from new considerations about academic integrity.

Overall, while AI technology can potentially be used to cheat with "lazy prompts" in any type of assessment, the vulnerability of each assessment depends on the nature of the assessment itself. Assessments that require the students to apply their knowledge and skills in a real-world setting, such as performance tasks and experiential learning, are less vulnerable. As previously mentioned, if AI proves useful in the "real world," who are we to constrain its utility in the academic realm?

Among alternatives, let us not fail to mention various tests and quizzes. A well-designed and appropriately used multiple-choice quiz can be very good at gauging student knowledge and skills. Employing a series of low-stakes quizzes throughout the term is more effective than relying on a single, high-stakes final exam. Short-answer quizzes can be very good at assessing student understanding of key concepts. As you will see a little later, AI can assist in designing better tests.

My core argument is this: As stewards of higher education, we should neither concede defeat nor forecast the end of our teaching methods simply because a chatbot can churn out a decent essay. Such a perspective oversimplifies a far more intricate reality. We are on the precipice of a transformation, but this change is not necessarily a downfall.

Indeed, the emergence of AI is a challenge, but it is also an opportunity, an impetus to reconsider and revamp our educational practices. The task is not to resist the tide of technology but to learn how to ride it, harnessing its strengths and mitigating its weaknesses. Moreover, we have the creativity to redesign our courses, assessments, and assignments in ways that leverage AI without compromising educational quality. We can use AI as a tool, not as a substitute, to support learning and to allow us to focus more on the tasks that truly require human judgment, such as fostering critical thinking, cultivating creativity, and nurturing ethical sensibility.

Crucially, our professional ethics serve as our North Star in this venture. They remind us that our goal is not just to produce competent writers but to educate responsible, thoughtful, and creative individuals. They instill in us the commitment to ensure that the rise of AI serves to enhance, not undermine, the richness and depth of university education.

While the trajectory of higher education in the AI era is unpredictable, it is anything but bleak. It calls for adaptation, not resignation. It demands that we, as educators, rise to the occasion and make university learning more meaningful, engaging, and enriching than ever before.

Instructional Design

In higher education, it is a disconcerting truth that many tasked with molding the minds of future generations often lack formal training in the art and science of teaching. As a result, the craft of imparting knowledge can devolve into a hit-or-miss endeavor, one predicated more on intuition or antiquated traditions than on empirically backed methodologies. The intense pressure to publish often eclipses the crucial role of effective teaching, particularly among faculty aspiring to secure tenure. When the scales tip too heavily toward research, it is the quality of teaching that endures the brunt of the neglect. The labor economics of universities make the problem worse by incentivizing the more and more extensive use of lecturers and student assistants for teaching assignments.

Such makeshift approaches might find purchase in elite bastions of learning, where the halls echo with the intellectual vigor of students arriving already equipped with a significant base of knowledge and motivation. But in institutions where underrepresented or first-generation students form a substantial portion, such a laissez-faire approach is utterly inadequate. According to data from the US Department of Education, a sobering 36% of students fail to graduate with a bachelor's degree within six years.[4] In many institutions, this percentage is much higher.

It is essential to highlight the growing concern among many universities, particularly those prioritizing accessibility, regarding high DFW (Dropout, Failure, Withdrawal) rates. These institutions bear witness to how such rates disproportionately impact students of color and first-generation college students, perpetuating existing societal disparities in educational attainment.

Consider that a large university campus might offer thousands of courses. Institutional research at these universities is usually capable of identifying a few specific courses that cater to many students and simultaneously demonstrate higher-than-normal DFW rates. Identifying these courses is a vital step in improving educational outcomes. However, the question of intervention—that is, what to do once these courses have been identified—remains fraught with uncertainties.

A particularly troubling aspect of this conundrum is the prevalence of educators who brandish a high failure rate as a badge of honor, seemingly a testament to their commitment to academic rigor. This mindset perpetuates an environment detrimental to the learning process. It falls upon the academic community to reassess and question whether the umbrella of academic freedom should extend to cover poor teaching practices and obsolete curricula.

As the college-going population expands, the demand for additional student support grows. Unfortunately, higher education faculty often lack the necessary training in instructional design and pedagogy, a situation that can be worsened by the misguided belief in "screening courses." This represents a significant problem.

Typically, course redesign falls within the expertise of instructional designers who collaborate with faculty to revise curriculum, pedagogy, and assessment practices. However, universities often grapple with a shortage of instructional designers, particularly those with broad and deep knowledge to assist faculty effectively in redesigning challenging courses across various disciplines. Mid-sized and large campuses usually have a center for teaching and learning, offering workshops, professional learning communities, and resources. Regrettably, these services are often utilized by instructors who already excel at teaching and wish to further enhance their skills. Those responsible for bottleneck courses rarely take advantage of these resources. It is a well-diagnosed, but poorly treated disease.

This is where AI-powered chatbots can prove to be a formidable solution. The nature of the problem makes it particularly suitable. How is a typical course designed? Pedagogues build on their predecessors' work and glean insights from more experienced colleagues. While a well-designed course may contain a spark of originality, it is usually the product of accumulated wisdom. Instructors often overlook aspects in their course design mainly because they are unaware of what others have done at different universities. Pedagogical knowledge struggles to accumulate, and this is where AI chatbots can excel. Drawing from the broad pool of pedagogical strategies and instructional designs, chatbots can assist in identifying gaps, suggesting improvements, and facilitating a more robust and effective course design.

To harness AI effectively for syllabus revision, faculty can begin with the skeleton of the course—the existing syllabus. This serves as fodder for the AI-powered chatbot, a rich prompt ripe for an analysis. From a critique of the syllabus' structure, content, and learning objectives, to suggesting potential improvements or identifying overlooked gaps, AI's capacity to analyze and provide feedback based on vast data repositories can be immensely helpful. Try a simple prompt: "Critique my syllabus with a particular focus on student engagement." Once ChatGPT or Claude gives its verdict, ask it for specific suggestions on all aspects of course design: learning outcomes, content, pacing, reading list, learning activities, assessments, and rubrics.

The more laborious facets of course design should not be overlooked. AI chatbots can offer entire templates for class activities and take-home assignments, recommend timelines for formative assessments, and assist in the structuring of course schedules. The purpose is not to blindly adopt AI-generated suggestions but to treat them as sparks for thought, as catalysts for revising and enhancing your syllabus.

Even if you have a lot of confidence in your current syllabus, submitting it to an AI-aided critique might yield unexpected benefits. It can infuse fresh elements into your course, stimulate new ways of thinking, or validate the strengths of your existing teaching methodology. If you are a true professional, you will not be afraid of some critique, especially if it is not public. The minimum you can do is to ask AI what it thinks about your syllabus. Think about this process as a kind of peer review. Indeed, behind ChatGPT's recommendations is the collective wisdom of your peers. The reason AI works so well in instructional design is that it is one of those fields where "the wisdom of the crowd" beats almost any individual mind, with the exception of a few top experts.

Numerous courses suffer from an austere "lecture-test" design—characterized by a lack of engaging learning activities and inadequate or non-existent formative assessments. Many professors aspire to engage their students but struggle to devise effective activities, thereby resorting to lecturing. With the assistance of AI, faculty can adopt a more engaging approach, enriching the learning experience and, in turn, transforming the educational landscape.

Bear in mind that AI encompasses all subjects, except for extremely niche, research-specific, graduate courses that delve into the frontiers of contemporary science. However, these courses seldom pose a problem. The primary areas of concern tend to be introductory courses, such as Biology 101 or Physics 201. For these foundational subjects, AI-powered chatbots can offer a wealth of creative strategies, all drawn from the collective wisdom of educators around the globe. As such, they can guide instructors in developing engaging activities, providing more effective feedback, and generally improving their pedagogical approach.

In many contexts, well-designed multiple-choice tests are applicable. Crafting a well-structured multiple-choice test is a task often met with trepidation by educators worldwide. The trickiest part is creating plausible distractors—incorrect options that must appear credible enough to challenge the students, yet not so misleading that they befuddle even the well-prepared individuals. The painstaking process of devising these false choices is time-consuming and let us admit, not very enjoyable. Here, AI comes to our aid, showcasing its potential to significantly streamline this process.

Crafting tests is a genre-specific type of writing, a domain where AI can truly shine. Given a dataset or study material, AI can formulate plausible questions and, in most instances, identify the correct answer. For more complex topics, human intervention might be necessary to guide the AI toward the right solution. Yet, the bulk of the task, including drafting distractors, can be managed efficiently by the AI.

Not stopping at mere question creation, AI's capabilities can be leveraged to add a level of complexity to your tests. Whether you need to elevate the difficulty to challenge your more advanced students or lower it for a foundational course, AI can accommodate these requests with ease. Moreover, AI can also help elevate the quality of the tests you create.

When constructing a test with AI assistance, it can provide an analysis of various psychometric characteristics of the test or another quantitative instrument, such as content validity, construct validity, and reliability. It can help you understand the test's difficulty level, discrimination power (the ability of a test item to differentiate among students based on how well they know the material), bias, and fairness. With some pilot data, AI can even run an item response analysis— a method used to improve the quality of tests by examining how different test items perform in a sample population. This level of refinement is often beyond the scope of what a typical course instructor might undertake and requires some training in psychometrics. However, with the help of AI, the basic analysis and improvement of measurements can be accomplished by anyone.

Another time-consuming element of course design is the evaluation rubric. Try a prompt like this to assess the potential of AI: "Turn this into a real rubric, with each of the indicators described at three levels—beginner, target, outstanding: Originality and freshness of the ideas (40%); Authentic, unique voice (30%); Taste, eloquence, appropriateness for target audience (30%)."

In summary, the potential of AI in the realm of course design is vast and yet to be fully tapped. As technology continues to evolve and become more sophisticated, the role of AI in education is expected to grow, shaping the future of teaching, and learning, in unimaginable ways.

While individual instructors can certainly utilize ChatGPT to redesign their courses independently, a more potent strategy would involve a coordinated institutional effort. This would entail organizing and incentivizing these redesign initiatives, involving instructional designers, and ensuring all problematic courses are addressed. Such an institutional approach, which marries human ingenuity with AI capabilities, is extremely promising. It symbolizes a significant stride toward alleviating high DFW rates and promoting a more inclusive and equitable education, especially for those most vulnerable to being marginalized. By adopting such a strategy, we can guarantee that all students, regardless of their background or chosen discipline, are provided with equal opportunities to succeed.

Grading

Remember that it was just two sections ago that I declared the traditional writing assignment to be trudging to extinction. With the reduced volume of such assignments, it is likely that the burdensome task of grading might also decrease, making way for other, less labor-intensive forms of evaluating student performance. However, the AI-assisted writing also needs to be graded. And even though the proposition sounds a bit absurd, AI is very good at evaluating the text produced in collaboration with itself. This is easy to test—just feed a chatbot with what you just produced with its help and ask to evaluate on certain criteria.

The sheer volume of similar projects makes grading laborious and, at times, monotonous. Sustaining attention and maintaining a high level of scrutiny become increasingly difficult as one navigates through the sea of student work. Additionally, the constraints of time further compound the problem. The brief windows typically allocated for grading, or "marking" as referred to in many other countries, mean professors often have to marathon through stacks of assignments, which can lead to fatigue and a dip in evaluation quality.

There are two kinds of assessments: Summative and formative. Summative feedback, while providing an endpoint evaluation, does not contribute as significantly to a student's ongoing learning journey. On the contrary, investing considerable time and effort in providing detailed feedback on students' final projects often proves counterproductive. Students, having reached the end of their project, are unlikely to thoroughly review or learn from this feedback. The fact that their final product is complete, and the feedback will not alter their grade, only adds to this lack of motivation.

In contrast, formative feedback—that which is given during the learning process—proves far more effective for student development. This involves providing critique and suggestions on drafts, proposals, and interim pieces of work. This form of feedback offers students an opportunity to make real-time improvements and solidifies their learning during the process of project completion. It allows them to understand their mistakes, correct them, and, most importantly, learn from them.

While pedagogically superior, formative feedback is a more substantial investment of an instructor's time. Each student's work requires individualized attention and personalized advice. Broad, general feedback is not as beneficial because it does not address the unique strengths and weaknesses of a student's work. Instead, formative feedback must be detailed and specific, homing in on individual areas for improvement and highlighting what the student has done well. This process, although time-consuming, can significantly enhance a student's learning experience and final work quality.

In other words, providing feedback is both the most valuable and the most time-consuming part of teaching. Instructors can and should be assisted with it.

Claude, a competitor to ChatGPT, is distinguished by its ability to handle a larger input size, a feature that provides it an edge over other AI-powered chatbots. Claude accepts not just a copy-pasted text but also documents in .doc, .pdf, and .txt formats. This capacity to process more extensive and diverse inputs empowers Claude to deliver better-informed responses, even though its output size remains constrained.

Using Claude for grading entails an upfront investment of time to create a detailed evaluation rubric. Rubrics have long played an essential role in education, acting as navigational beacons that guide students toward understanding the expectations and standards of quality work. Yet, for an AI like Claude, a rubric is not merely beneficial—it is vital. Claude evaluates any text-based student work in accordance with this rubric, allotting points based on the predefined benchmarks. To make this work, simply upload both the student's work and the rubric, then instruct Claude about the kind of feedback you need. Do not restrict yourself to only asking for grades, but also request individualized written feedback and specific suggestions. Providing that you check every single word of the feedback manually, Claude becomes an asset in not just assessing, but also enhancing, the learning process.

Of course, the utility of Claude may have its limitations. If you are teaching a course with a heavy emphasis on creativity and individual style, such as a Master of Fine Arts (MFA) course in scriptwriting, Claude may not be the most suitable tool. However, it may still be worth a try, as AI continues to evolve and surprise us with its capabilities. For most university courses, particularly those with a large text-based evaluation component, Claude can offer substantial benefits, streamlining the grading process and offering consistent, unbiased evaluations.

As we continue to embrace AI's role in the realm of education, particularly in grading and providing feedback on student work, it is crucial to acknowledge and address the ethical considerations that arise. A key question that emerges is whether it is ethical to pass off AI-generated feedback as our own. I will discuss the ethics of authorship later in the book, but here is a suggestion for the context of grading. Transparency regarding the grading process is essential, and presenting AI-generated feedback as human-generated feedback is not recommended. Honesty is the best policy. However, if your process involves 100% manual checking and editing of what AI drafted for you, the details of the process must not necessarily be disclosed. In a way, the principle is like any other authored writing: if you use AI for drafting, but retain a full responsibility for releasing the output, it is your business how you arrived at the final draft. Passing raw AI-generated content without your review is deceptive.

In many instances, empowering students with the skills to self-assess their work using AI tools like Claude might prove more valuable. Allowing students to continuously review and grade their drafts affords them the opportunity to refine their work until they achieve their full potential. I would recommend training students to handle two tasks: firstly, to receive critical feedback from Claude guided by your rubric, and, secondly, to instruct Claude to revise based on alterations in the prompt. By doing so, students will be equipped to produce their best work, aided by a powerful tool.

If you empower students to self-grade their drafts, consider reserving human intervention for crucial phases of the learning process. At the start of a project, during the brainstorming and conceptualization stages, human guidance can help shape the trajectory of student work. This is an often-neglected step. Student work may not be strong because their main idea is weak. Investing more time in helping them to generate a good key idea may be worth it. Once the work is complete, human evaluators can step in again to not only assess the final product but also engage the students in a reflective conversation about their learning journey. This approach allows for a balanced integration of AI capabilities and human expertise, capitalizing on the strengths of both.

The shift toward AI assistance in grading introduces a new dynamic, one that resembles tutoring, which I will discuss in the next section. Nevertheless, a balance between AI and human feedback seems to be the most effective strategy. Students might question the value of a course if the instructor's role appears minimal. It is vital to remember that the final responsibility for assessing and educating students still rests with the human instructor. Ideally, educators should spend less time on routine tasks like grading for technical skills, and more time on building relationships with students, understanding their individual levels of knowledge and skills, gauging their motivations, and providing guidance and coaching. AI can efficiently handle more routine grading tasks, freeing up time for educators to focus on these more complex aspects of teaching.

AI's potential extends to support the efforts of teaching assistants who are often charged with the task of grading and providing feedback. By integrating AI into their workflow, teaching assistants can enhance their efficiency and effectiveness. They could employ AI to produce initial evaluations or grading, while maintaining their crucial role in reviewing the AI's outputs for precision, relevance, and appropriateness.

Consider a scenario in a large lecture course where multiple short-answer questions require grading. In such a context, teaching assistants could harness AI to assist in the initial grading. The AI could provide a preliminary evaluation of the answers, and then the teaching assistant would be able to review, modify, and adjust as necessary. This method combines the processing power of AI with the nuanced understanding and judgment of a human grader.

Claude's exceptional capabilities in analyzing extensive texts present a unique opportunity to enhance learning analytics. Let us envision a scenario where you download threaded conversations or compile an entire class's essays or precis into one document. You could then feed this data to Claude and inquire— what concepts and skills should I focus on? Where are the gaps in my students' understanding in this specific class? This presents an unparalleled chance for the implementation of formative assessment in higher education, a concept that emphasizes regular feedback and adjustments in teaching and learning.

Tutoring and Self-help

Academic Tutoring

I called upon ChatGPT to assess my skills in German and Spanish, specifically in grammar and vocabulary. It instantaneously devised tests and evaluated my responses with notable expertise. Within a span of ten minutes, I had a comprehensive view of my current proficiency in these languages. ChatGPT gave me detailed feedback, pinpointing my correct responses and areas requiring further attention. Following this, I inquired, "Could you explain the subjunctive mood in Spanish, and does it have counterparts in English, German, or Russian?" The explanation it furnished, complete with examples in those familiar languages, was excellent. I then asked for a series of exercises to polish my Spanish grammar. Contrasting this experience with the tedious nature of traditional language textbooks, I felt as if I had entered an entirely new realm of learning.

Keep in mind that this capability extends beyond language learning and can be applied to virtually any discipline. For instance, I requested an example of how Mikhail Bakhtin's concept of polyphony could be applied to educational theory—a topic not typically encountered in standard college curricula. ChatGPT provided a reasonable example. While it was not groundbreaking or exceptionally creative, it was accurate and sensible, a solid foundation upon which further ideas could be constructed.

Dear college professor, choose a concept that your students often struggle to grasp, and ask an AI-powered chatbot for an explanation. Request examples as well. Evaluate the quality of the explanation, and then ask for 20 more explanations and 20 additional examples. Reflect on this—do you have the bandwidth or patience to provide this level of detail for every one of your students? If the answer is no, you might want to recommend AI chatbots as personal tutors for your students.

I understand that some applications of AI-powered chatbots proposed in this book may provoke controversy. Nevertheless, their use for personal tutoring is broadly accepted and, in my view, foolproof. No valid arguments against such usage exist. In medical research, some trials are halted prematurely because the benefits of a new medication are so compelling that it is deemed unethical to continue the trial, thereby delaying the new drug's availability to all patients. We are almost there with the use of AI for individual tutoring. Our profession may reasonably need time to consider the idea of writing with AI or feel hesitant about using AI to generate class assignments. However, failing to encourage students to use chatbots for individual tutoring could arguably be seen as an ethical failure rather than a reasonable caution at this point.

At the core of education lies a dilemma. The most transformative gift we can bestow upon our students is the benefit of individual attention, a currency which we often find ourselves in short supply. Ideally, we should provide each student with a personal tutor—an ally in learning—to cater to their unique pace and preferences outside the classroom. This proposition, no matter how appealing, has been largely economically implausible. With AI, we may be on the cusp of taking a big step closer to this educational utopia. The AI-powered tools can serve as personal tutors in the modern educational landscape, providing individualized attention to students.

The effectiveness of an AI tutor fundamentally stems from its adaptability to diverse learning styles and individual needs. If a student struggles to comprehend a concept at the first attempt, the AI tutor can nimbly adjust its explanatory strategy, re-framing the concept in a new light. The AI's limitless patience and vast array of explanations extinguish any fear of appearing unintelligent or irritating by asking "too many" questions. This aspect is especially beneficial for first-generation students or those who tend to be less assertive or communicative. What we are discussing here is more than just a matter of convenience. Thanks to AI, we are witnessing the democratization of personalized tutoring, a privilege traditionally available only to a fortunate minority. This evolution could dramatically decrease the socio-economic disparity in education, paving the way for universally accessible, high-quality educational support.

Extensive use of AI for tutoring brings closer a shift in the educator's role from a knowledge dispenser, repeating the same content to different groups of students, to a more nuanced role as a learning facilitator. This shift allows educators to focus on individual needs, catering to specific difficulties that students might encounter with course content. As a result, classrooms can evolve into environments where learning is not just imparted but also personalized, which could potentially enhance students' understanding and engagement.

An AI tutor may occasionally struggle to navigate the complexities of advanced graduate courses or the nuances of cutting-edge theories, as the knowledge base grounding their training data does not necessarily extend into these specialized areas. Current AI language models suffer from the problem of hallucinations (when plausible information is equated with factual information). However, these constraints do not detract from their valuable role in helping students with foundational subjects, areas like statistics, mathematics, writing, and economics where assistance is often needed most. This risk of an occasional error should be compared against realistic alternatives. The potential pitfalls of not offering tutoring at all or relying on inconsistent peer tutoring are generally greater. The risks associated with AI tutors can be mitigated by informing instructors and students of these limitations, while highlighting their benefits.

It is incumbent upon us as educators to not only provide our students with this innovative tool but also teach them how to use it effectively. We need to guide them toward seeking AI's help in understanding concepts, rather than merely generating solutions. The focus should be on comprehension and mastery rather than on the completion of a task.

This shift in perspective is crucial. Instead of asking AI to solve a math problem, students should ask it to explain the steps involved in solving it. They should persist with questions until they understand the concept and the logic behind the solution. It is not enough to just tell students that chatbots are out there, and they are good personal tutors. I would recommend investing some of the class time into demonstrating how to make a chatbot useful. Consider giving students at least the start by something like this:

When using an AI like ChatGPT as a personal tutor for a college class, the most effective prompts will vary based on the topic and the individual's study needs. Here are some general prompts that can guide students:

1. **Conceptual Understanding:** Students can ask to explain or simplify complex concepts.
   —"Can you explain the concept of supply and demand in economics?"
   —"What is the Pythagorean Theorem, and can you give examples of how to use it?"
2. **Homework Assistance:** Ask for help in solving homework problems.
   —"How do I solve this calculus problem: integral of sin(x) dx from 0 to pi?"
   —"Could you help me outline an essay on the causes of World War II?"
3. **Theory Application:** Request examples of how theories or concepts apply in real-world scenarios.
   —"Can you give an example of how the prisoner's dilemma is applied in real life?"
   —"How does Freud's theory of psychoanalysis apply in contemporary psychology?"
4. **Review and Quizzes:** Generate quizzes or review questions for self-study.
   —"Can you generate a quiz for me on the Periodic Table of Elements?"
   —"Can you provide review questions for the French Revolution?"
5. **Discussion and Argument Construction:** Use ChatGPT to help construct arguments for essays or participate in discussions.
   —"Can you help me form an argument for the benefits of renewable energy sources?"
   —"What are the key arguments against universal basic income?"
6. **Study Strategies:** Get suggestions on effective study strategies.
   —"What are effective strategies for studying for a biology final exam?"
   —"How can I better memorize vocabulary for a foreign language?"

It is crucial to reemphasize that the accessibility of AI-powered chatbots presents a question of equity. These technological resources will predominantly assist those who are actively invited and motivated to utilize them. Therefore, we must endeavor to ensure that students from less advantaged backgrounds receive equivalent access and encouragement to these tools, on par with their more privileged counterparts.

While we are not quite at the stage where AI can replace human advisors, there is promising potential for using AI in academic advising. Now, there is limited evidence to suggest that existing AI models can offer accurate advice to students. I tested ChatGPT and Claude on their ability to help students construct a semester schedule based on the student's transcript and the catalog. Both produced too many errors for this use to be immediately useful. However, this is likely to change as technology advances.

Academic advising often involves interpreting complex regulations and guidelines and translating them into more digestible, human-friendly advice. This is precisely the kind of logical task that AI excels at. With improvements, AI could potentially handle the bulk of the information-gathering and interpretation, allowing human advisors to focus on more nuanced, emotional aspects of student guidance.

Coaching

In many professional programs—ranging from teaching and counseling to communications, medicine, law, and social work—students primarily develop their skills through instructor feedback. This is a time-honored pedagogical method: A seasoned professional observes a student's practice, either in real time or via recorded media like video, and provides detailed feedback for improvement. Typically, a mentor or an instructor observes a student's practice session. In the context of teaching, for instance, an experienced educator might attend a student teacher's class, taking notes on teaching methods, class engagement, and the effectiveness of the lesson plan. Following the observation, the mentor provides constructive feedback, often aligning it with a specific evaluation rubric for more precision. Human observations are time-consuming and costly, especially when scaled across multiple students and multiple observation points. All one-on-one instruction is very expensive.

AI-powered chatbots offer an intriguing alternative. Imagine a student teacher's lesson being transcribed in real time and analyzed by an AI like ChatGPT or Claude. The AI could focus on various aspects of the teaching session, from the teacher's speech patterns and clarity to the structure of the lesson itself.

What makes this even more interesting is the ability to input a specific evaluation rubric into the AI. This enables the AI to align its feedback more closely with program-specific goals and evaluation criteria, making the feedback more targeted and, therefore, more actionable for the student.

Initial experiments in using AI for feedback on transcribed student performance have yielded promising results. Particularly, AI tools have proven to be adept at recognizing and analyzing speech patterns and structures. While this does not replace the nuanced understanding and experience a human mentor brings to the table, it offers a valuable supplement. The AI-generated feedback can provide a different, more data-driven perspective that might highlight areas a human mentor could overlook.

Moreover, the AI's feedback can be generated far more quickly and at a lower cost than traditional methods. This could allow for more frequent evaluations, providing students with more opportunities for growth and improvement. For example, I sometimes record my own public talk or a meeting that I facilitate, and ask AI to give me feedback on my performance. It produces meaningful and mostly accurate feedback.

It is worth noting that, while AI offers many advantages, there are ethical considerations to be aware of. Data privacy is paramount, especially in settings like counseling or medical training. It is still not clear to what degree chat data is anonymized in the process of AI training. Further, relying solely on AI feedback could miss out on the qualitative, human elements that often make education in professional programs so impactful. Therefore, AI should serve as an augmentation to human feedback, rather than a replacement.

Although we are far from the day when AI can fully replace human mentors in professional education, the technology has evolved to a point where it can significantly augment traditional methods. By using AI to analyze practice sessions based on specific evaluation criteria, professional programs can offer a more efficient, data-driven feedback loop that complements the indispensable insights provided by human mentors. This not only stands to benefit the next generation of professionals but also could make high-quality education more accessible and affordable.

Mental Self-help

Another intriguing application is in mental health support. However, this sector comes with its own set of challenges, primarily around data privacy and ownership. Currently, there is a lack of clarity on who owns the data that is input into AI-powered chatbots and what measures are in place to secure this sensitive information. Until these concerns are adequately addressed, the deployment of AI in this area will remain limited.

That said, my experience testing ChatGPT in general mental health-related conversations suggests that AI can offer some level of support. While it is crucial to emphasize that AI chatbots are not substitutes for professional mental health treatment, they can engage in meaningful conversations and provide basic advice. For example, ChatGPT suggested strategies for a struggling student on how to ask for help or approach a professor or an advisor. It even offered a hypothetical role-playing exercise to help the student overcome the fear of asking for help.

In summary, while we are not yet at a point where AI can completely take over roles in academic advising or mental health support, technology does show promise. Logical tasks, such as deciphering complex academic regulations, are well within the realm of what AI can handle efficiently. As for mental health applications, once the issues surrounding data privacy and ownership are resolved, AI has the potential to offer meaningful support. However, until then, human expertise and ethical considerations will continue to take precedence.

Notes

1 *Future of Work Report*, LinkedIn, August 2023, 17, https://economicgraph.linkedin.com/content/dam/me/economicgraph/en-us/PDF/future-of-work-report-ai-august-2023.pdf

2 John Hattie, *Visible Learning: A Synthesis of over 800 Meta-analyses Relating to Achievement* (Routledge, 2008).
3 See the foundational Joy Paul Guilford, "The Structure of Intellect," *Psychological Bulletin* 53, no. 4 (1956): 267.
4 National Center for Education Statistics, "Undergraduate Graduation Rates," https://nces.ed.gov/fastfacts/display.asp?id=40

3   Scholarship

In this chapter, we explore the use of AI in research and scholarly activities. The incorporation of AI in these fields is a pursuit of efficiency, a means to enhance productivity, and a powerful tool for overcoming challenges such as writer's block, procrastination, or the daunting prospect of facing a blank page. All you need is a single idea, and an AI chatbot can help transform it into a short text, an outline, or a literature search, making that initial step less overwhelming.

However, it is crucial to remain cognizant of both the strengths and limitations of AI-powered chatbot technology. This awareness ensures that we are not disillusioned by unrealistic expectations or overly captivated by technology's allure. Ideally, AI should amplify our research output capability without detracting from the inherent joy and curiosity that drive the process of inquiry.

Throughout this chapter, I will discuss and demonstrate various ways AI tools can streamline research processes, provide insights into data, and assist with writing and editing. Just to be clear, my scope of vision includes mostly humanities, social sciences, and professional fields. Some of my advice may be more or less useful to scholars from other disciplines such as natural sciences, mathematics and computer science, engineering, and others.

The Wisdom of the Digital Crowd

What is the role of AI in generating new ideas? To understand this better, let us view AI chatbots as a digital "crowd." This is linked to their training mechanisms. They learn from a wide array of text data from the internet, encapsulating an expansive range of knowledge and perspectives. When interacting with a chatbot, you are dealing with a system that mirrors the collective wisdom and potential errors found in its crowd-sourced training data.

The "wisdom of the crowd" as a principle came from Sir Francis Galton's experiment in 1907. Galton, at a country fair, invited attendees to guess the weight of an ox. While individual guesses varied significantly, the average of all these estimates surprisingly landed extremely close to the actual weight of the ox. This experiment demonstrated how collective wisdom could harness the diverse perspectives of a crowd to reach an astonishingly accurate result.[1]

DOI: 10.4324/9781032686028-3

A modern manifestation of this collective wisdom unfolds every day in the global financial markets. These markets are arenas where the aggregate intelligence of thousands of investors, each with unique perspectives and insights, continuously determines the pricing of securities. Even though occasional anomalies like market bubbles and crashes occur, the market, over time, demonstrates remarkable efficiency in asset pricing. This efficiency emerges from the crowd's wisdom, an uncoordinated coalescence of a vast array of information.

In both examples, whether in Galton's country fair or in the contemporary financial markets, the wisdom of the crowd proves its worth. It surfaces the common knowledge among the diversity, validating the concept that an informed crowd can provide surprisingly accurate and efficient solutions. As we turn our gaze toward AI-powered chatbots, we must remember that they, like the crowds, can harness and amplify this collective wisdom, aiding us in our journey of ideation and creativity.

On the other hand, crowds can also be alarmingly misguided at times. An example is panic buying, often seen during crises like the COVID-19 pandemic, when crowds of people, driven by fear and uncertainty, stockpile goods leading to shortages. This behavior, while individually rational, can lead to collectively detrimental outcomes, a phenomenon known as the tragedy of the commons.[2] Similarly, we have seen how crowds can be manipulated by misinformation, particularly on social media, leading to harmful social and political outcomes. When your AI friend starts "hallucinating," that is generating plausible but false content, consider it to be the other side of the wisdom of the crowd.

The novelty of an idea is evaluated based on its comparison to pre-existing concepts. It is impossible to assert an idea as new or develop it into a cohesive concept without an understanding of existing scholarship. This is where AI truly shines in the brainstorming process—it conserves time by helping to grasp and encapsulate the current body of knowledge.

Suppose you are on the brink of what you believe is a breakthrough concept. AI has honed its capacity to comprehend and evaluate your proposed concept, even in its embryonic stage. Through its pattern recognition and flexible keyword matching abilities, the AI can scour through massive repositories of information and determine if your idea, or something akin to it, has been proposed before, and if yes, under which names?

Furthermore, AI's knowledge extends across interdisciplinary boundaries, providing you with insights gleaned from research in fields that may not be directly related to your own. In our era of vast and ever-expanding scholarship, it is a formidable task for an individual to stay updated on more than a handful of specific domains. In contrast, AI has the capacity to survey a broader landscape of knowledge, providing a comprehensive perspective that helps prevent unnecessary replication of pre-existing ideas.

Ultimately, writing, particularly in the academic sphere, is rarely a concentrated outpouring of entirely original ideas. More often, it involves restating, recontextualizing, and building upon what is already known. This process provides the backdrop against which your novel ideas can shine. The AI-powered chatbots, with their ability to efficiently retrieve and present established knowledge, serve as excellent partners in this journey. By taking on the job of providing context, and restating what already has been established, AI can significantly increase research output.

However, the efficacy of AI diminishes when the task calls for stepping beyond the confines of common knowledge or traditional thought paradigms. Although AI can discern the novelty of an idea, generating a truly novel idea is not its forte. Sure, you might occasionally witness an unexpected spark of what looks like creativity, but these instances are exceptions rather than the rule.

Indeed, there is a surprising element of creativity that thrives on the random and spontaneous revelation of new patterns. AI can occasionally stumble upon an innovative perspective, much like an unexpectedly good verse of poetry might emerge amidst numerous fruitless attempts. While these instances are rare and more the result of serendipity than skill, they remind us of the potential hidden within the vast realms of AI.

AI chatbots excel in domains where the wisdom of crowds thrives, retrieving known facts, understanding established thought patterns, and interpreting the conventions of various disciplines. However, they falter when tasked with transcending common knowledge to generate original insights. Like a crowd reciting known facts not necessarily producing a groundbreaking theory, AI chatbots currently cannot reliably yield novel ideas. Nonetheless, humans can more readily generate such new ideas when they can rely on AI to construct the foundational background that triggers original thoughts.

Turbocharging Search

Human memory can be fallible, as evidenced by my recent struggle to recall the name of the economist W.J. Baumol and his theory of "cost disease," a concept I am well-versed in and even wrote a paper on just a few years ago. However, AI like ChatGPT can bridge these gaps, providing information when memory fails. For example, when I asked ChatGPT about the theorist who suggested productivity does not increase in theater compared to other industries, it reminded me of Baumol's name.

In another instance, despite being an applied philosopher, I find the history of philosophy rather tedious. Yet, acknowledging key names who have thought about similar problems is common practice in the field. I utilized my AI chatbot companion, asking it, "Which philosophers believed that human ignorance is the main source of evil?" While I was aware of Socrates' thinking on the matter, I did not want to miss any other prominent names. OK, it was Hobbes and Kant; of course, I knew that, especially after the reminder.

The utility of AI chatbots also extends to situations where we grapple with our own memory's limitations. We have all experienced those moments when we recall the gist of an idea from a classical text but struggle to find the exact citation or to remember the correct author. Often, our memory embellishes the idea with non-existent details or erroneously assigns it to a different author. In such situations, AI-powered chatbots can be instrumental in retrieving the precise information. They can sift through vast databases of knowledge to locate the specific citation or text you are seeking, even if they may not succeed on the first attempt.

One of AI's most incredible capacities is its ability to identify and cluster similar ideas. Scholars are well familiar with this scenario: trying to articulate a concept, all while uncertain if it has already been addressed in existing literature, only under a different name. Traditionally, the primary hurdle with search engines has been identifying the precise terms that best encapsulate your idea or query. As groundbreaking as Google search was, one needed to be well-versed in a specific field to recognize an idea expressed in different terms and to know which terms are used in that field.

In sociological studies, the term "social capital" is commonly used, whereas, in business and organization theory, this concept often goes by the name "networking." Similarly, "structural violence," a term predominantly used in peace studies and conflict resolution, corresponds closely to what sociology and law often refer to as "systemic discrimination."

However, AI can effortlessly surmount this obstacle. It does not need to know the exact words or terms. Through intricate algorithms and nuanced understanding of semantics, AI can intuitively grasp the essence of an idea and find correlating information. Let us delve into an example to clarify:

Imagine posing the question, "Is there a concept or theory that would measure the density of thought per unit of text? In other words, certain texts may be extensive yet carry very few actual ideas, while others may be more condensed, teeming with insights and arguments. Is there an index that quantifies this?"

Such a question requires a comprehensive understanding of the topic to find relevant literature effectively. Inputting a simplified version of this query into a traditional search engine may not yield the results you are seeking. However, AI, using advanced language processing capabilities, can understand the nuance in the question. It can extract the underlying concept of measuring "idea density" in texts, even without having a predefined term for it.

ChatGPT:

There is not a universally recognized or standardized measure for the "density of thought" or idea content in a piece of text. The complexity and abstraction of ideas can make it very difficult to quantify in a precise way. However, several related concepts and theories could be useful for qualitatively discussing or comparing the idea density in different texts.

1. **Information Density**: This is a concept in linguistics which refers to the amount of information conveyed in the words or syllables of a given language. Different languages have different information densities. This is

not exactly what you are asking for, but it is a similar concept in that it involves the idea of "packing" information into language.

2. **Lexical Density**: This refers to the proportion of content words (nouns, verbs, adjectives, and adverbs) to the total number of words in a text. Texts with a higher proportion of content words are considered to have higher lexical density and are often more information-dense and complex.

3. **Readability Indexes**: These are formulas used to estimate the difficulty of reading a text. They usually consider factors like sentence length and syllable count. Although not directly measuring idea density, they could be indirectly related as texts with many complex ideas are likely to have lower readability scores. Some examples are the Flesch-Kincaid Readability Tests or the Gunning Fog Index.

4. **Topic Modeling**: This is a type of statistical model used in natural language processing to discover the abstract "topics" that occur in a collection of documents. It does not provide a simple numeric measure of idea density, but it could help identify and compare the number and variety of ideas in different texts.

Again, none of these concepts or techniques provides a straightforward measure of the density of thought or ideas in a text, as you are asking for. That kind of measure would likely require a deeper understanding of language and thought than current science allows. Nevertheless, these related concepts might provide useful ways to compare the complexity and content of different texts.

The advent of AI fundamentally transforms how we search for and engage with information, transcending the traditional limitations imposed by keyword-based searches. Gone are the days when mastery over specific search terms determined the success of academic reviews or interdisciplinary exchanges. AI's capabilities to explore databases, scholarly articles, and reference works allow for the identification of related concepts and theories, thus enriching our understanding and creating a more comprehensive knowledge landscape.

This technological leap is not confined to academic circles but extends across various fields. In healthcare, AI's advanced pattern recognition can aid in diagnosing patient symptoms more accurately. In law enforcement, AI can cross-reference case details with historical data, potentially expediting investigations.

AI also becomes a powerful ally when dealing with forgotten or imprecise ideas. Whether it is recalling a vaguely remembered theory or navigating an unfamiliar discipline, AI's extensive database access and rapid information processing can fill the gaps in our understanding with remarkable efficiency. Consider misquoting a famous saying; while traditional search engines might have faltered, AI can infer the gist of your recollection and provide the accurate quote.

Thus, AI's capacity for nuanced information retrieval is revolutionizing our engagement with knowledge. It lifts the burdensome need for precise term recall, allowing us to approach knowledge exploration more intuitively. AI fills in our memory gaps, effectively becoming an external extension of our cognitive processes, and thereby redefining our relationship with information in a more human-compatible manner.

Literature Reviews

In this section, we delve into the evolving role of literature reviews in academic research, particularly given the influence of AI and sophisticated search platforms like Google Scholar. Traditional methodologies for conducting literature reviews are undergoing significant transformation, requiring both students and faculty to adapt their skills continuously to stay abreast of these changes.

What makes a good literature review? A good literature review is more than a summary of existing work; it tells a story, identifying patterns, developments, strengths, and blind spots within the body of literature. It should be grounded in prior research while also identifying a gap that your own research fills. A successful review is clearly organized, has a strong voice, and does not read like an encyclopedia entry. The worst kinds of reviews are laundry lists: "so and so said this and that."

A good review should touch on foundational literature to position itself within scholarly traditions and should also highlight current trends if relevant. It is important to ensure you are not simply duplicating previous work and not overlooking relevant research due to differences in terminology. Consider organizing your literature review section like a mini-research project, with the subject being the body of literature you are reviewing. Begin by explaining how you selected the literature, how you reviewed it, and what your main claim or thesis is.

The review should then outline the main scholarly traditions that have influenced your own research and explain how these different traditions have considered similar phenomena but might have achieved different insights or have different limitations. It is crucial to articulate how your own work interacts with these traditions and contributes something new to the field.

To clarify, AI is not yet capable of independently producing a high-quality literature review, but it can generate a decent draft. Notably, AI ensures that significant figures and influential theories are not overlooked. The most common and embarrassing shortcoming of a literature review is missing a major contributor. This is something a chatbot would never do. It may miss smaller details, but it will identify a scholar who is extensively written about and frequently cited on a specific topic.

It is important to recognize that often the only individuals who read a scholarly paper from beginning to end are peer reviewers and journal editors. Other researchers typically employ varied strategies for quickly digesting the information within a paper, ranging from reading the abstract and possibly the literature review to scrutinizing the methodology and examining the findings. In some instances, there might even be situations where a less scrupulous researcher cites a paper or book without fully reading it. However, this problem precedes the AI age.

Excluding those who reference work without fully reading it, most scholars develop the essential skill of effectively skimming through research materials— a proficiency that tends to develop with experience. I anticipate that AI, like Claude, will revolutionize this process, establishing a new genre of enhanced research reading due to its ability to absorb and analyze extensive texts. For instance, Claude can be instructed to read a paper and summarize the main arguments, evaluate the methodology, or determine the paper's relevance to your own work. Although this book primarily focuses on "wraiting," a new form of writing, it is likely that AI will similarly transform the way we read. Essentially, AI can produce instant, customized "cliff notes" of research literature for specific purposes. These summaries go beyond the author-created abstracts but still make reading scholarly literature much more efficient.

This evolving landscape points to the potential benefits and challenges of integrating AI into the literature review process. AI's ability to rapidly analyze and synthesize vast amounts of data can revolutionize the practice, but it also raises new questions about best practices for conducting rigorous, comprehensive, and insightful reviews. As AI becomes more integral to the research process, I would not be surprised if the content we include in literature reviews also changes. Presently, for well-researched and well-published topics, AI can create a reasonably good draft of a literature review. In the past, authors sifted through hundreds of abstracts and conducted complex searches to compile a literature review. Now, it is more efficient to ask AI to draft a review, then read the sources it suggests, and subsequently correct, edit, or enhance the AI-generated review.

To achieve the detailed level of review, AI might not be fully proficient yet, but it can aid you in completing a significant portion of the task, maybe a third or even half of it, which is considerably beneficial. To advance further, revert to the principle of rich prompts. Your prompt could be structured like this:

> Compose a review of the research literature concerning student-teacher relationships within the fields of educational research and psychology. Specifically, highlight the measurement instruments that have been developed to date, and identify any gaps which may necessitate the creation of new instruments. Highlight the foundational authors in this field and their key contributions. Conclude with a list of references in APA style.

As with many tasks, the reliability of AI output decreases when dealing with increasingly narrow or specialized fields of study. There likely exists a point of diminishing returns, where manually conducting a review and simply using an

AI like ChatGPT or Claude to ensure nothing significant was overlooked prove to be easier. It is crucial to bear in mind the two main ways of interacting with AI: one is instructing the AI to perform a task; the other is soliciting its feedback on the work you have already completed.

The issue of accurate referencing remains a significant limitation for AI in academic contexts. While AIs like ChatGPT and Claude can format citations impeccably, they can generate fictitious but plausible references, known as "AI hallucinations." As Ben Lutkevich notes, these models lack an "understanding of the underlying reality that language describes,"[3] making them prone to produce a text that seems credible but is not. This is a sobering realization that points out a major limitation of large language model AI.

The risk of AI hallucinations in academia is high, as they undermine research credibility and can propagate misinformation. This calls for a dual approach: Developers should aim to improve AI's "fact-checking" capabilities, while users, especially in academia, must exercise due diligence in verifying AI-generated references. This collaborative effort is essential for the responsible integration of AI into academic practices.

Consequently, the responsibility of manually checking—and reading—all scholarly references still falls on the researcher. In this context, the role of AI tools like Claude and ChatGPT is to assist in gathering and generating references. However, the ultimate verification of these references remains within the researcher's purview.

Qualitative Research

In this section, we will look at how AI can help with tasks like analyzing data in research projects. Claude is still better at this than GPT 3.5 or 4 because it can handle longer texts. ChatGPT 4.0 has made significant progress in increasing the size of input.

For example, I used Claude to analyze a really long conversation that was more than 14,000 words. I got the edited version of this conversation from the Otter software and used it for my analysis. I asked Claude to do two things: first, to find the main topics talked about and how often they came up; second, to use a specific way of analyzing called grounded theory.

The results were good but not mind-blowing. Claude did a great job finding patterns in the text. Specifically, the conversation was about using AI in education, and Claude made a detailed list of main points about that topic:

- Student perspectives on using ChatGPT: 4
- Ethics and risks of ChatGPT: 8
- Impact on jobs and workforce: 6
- Regulation and policy: 5
- Integration into curriculum: 4
- Detecting ChatGPT-generated work: 3
- Role of humanities and critical thinking: 4

For those who have experienced the labor-intensive process of manual or semi-manual coding of ethnographic data, the timesaving capabilities of AI in this domain would be a significant advantage. This form of an AI-assisted analysis could eliminate numerous hours of meticulous work, traditionally required to sift through complex layers of data and identify patterns.

It is important to note that AI, in its current state, is not likely to replace a trained qualitative researcher entirely. The depth and nuance a human researcher brings to the table, particularly in identifying sophisticated codes or making sense of complex human behaviors and interactions, are still unmatched. However, the AI's contribution as an initial data filter is undeniable. It offers a robust starting point for researchers, quickly identifying and organizing basic themes and patterns in the data, thereby giving researchers a head start.

Another considerable benefit of AI in qualitative research is its ability to perform multiple rounds of data analysis. This is particularly valuable when researchers want to probe deeper into specific themes or concepts. For instance, in my experiment, I asked Claude to count and list the frequency of words associated with "anxiety" within the conversation. Within seconds, the AI generated an accurate tally. This immediate response time and precision can significantly enhance the efficiency and depth of a qualitative data analysis:

Here are the words related to anxiety and their frequencies in the conversation transcript:

- Concern/concerns/concerning: 8
- Worry/worrying: 2
- Fear: 1
- Scary: 2
- Threat: 1
- Risks: 5
- Existential risk: 2
- Pessimistic: 3
- Catastrophic: 2

The most common anxiety-related word was "concern" and its variants, which appeared 8 times. Other notable anxiety-related words were "risks" (5 times), "scary" (2 times), and "catastrophic" (2 times). The low overall frequency of explicitly anxiety-connoting words suggests the conversation maintained a calm, rational tone even when discussing potentially worrying implications of generative AI. But the concerns were still present in the discussion, if not always overtly emotional.

Indeed, the capabilities of AI can be quite remarkable when it comes to assisting with tasks traditionally conducted by humans. But AI really begins to shine in more complex tasks, such as applying the grounded theory methodology to analyze texts. Let us delve into the findings from the second experiment:

> Here is an analysis of the key themes in the conversation using the grounded theory approach:
> The overarching theme that emerges is the need to shape the development and use of generative AI like ChatGPT in a responsible way. This theme connects to several sub-themes:
>
> - Managing risks and ethics: There is significant concern about the potential risks and ethical implications of AI like ChatGPT, including issues like privacy, accountability, monopolization of knowledge production, and existential threats. This suggests the need for thoughtful governance and guardrails.
> - Preparing students and the workforce: Participants recognize the need to evolve curricula and opportunities to ensure students develop relevant skills and mindsets to contribute meaningfully with AI. This includes incorporating AI experiences into programs and reinventing humanities education.
> - Policy and regulation: Slow policy response compared to the pace of AI development is a problem. There are calls for more conversation between industry, government, and the public to get ahead of challenges.
> - Protecting rights and values: Beyond policy, there is a sense that scientists, universities, and the public need to steer the development of AI in a way that protects human rights, values, accountability, and diversity.
> - Maintaining human creativity: Concern that AI could displace creative professions, and a belief that the uniquely human element of creativity must be protected and valued.
> - Detection and plagiarism: Developing more robust detection of AI-generated text is needed to maintain academic integrity. But this is part of a larger cultural issue around incentives and integrity.
>
> The core category that connects these sub-themes is the need for intentional, ethical co-evolution of humans and AI systems, which respects human rights and values. This is the overarching grounded theory that emerges from the analysis of the conversation.

Certainly, while a seasoned researcher might deliver a more nuanced analysis, the crux of the matter is not about whether Claude outperforms a PhD-trained expert in qualitative research. The real question is: can an expert researcher accomplish more, and do it faster, with the assistance of AI like Claude?

The evidence, in my view, leans decidedly in favor of using AI for a text-based qualitative data analysis. While we may have varying opinions about whether AI brings us halfway or merely a quarter of the way, it is hard to dispute that the efficiency gains offered by AI are substantial and hence too significant to disregard.

When considering the use of AI-powered chatbots, it is crucial to align their application with their inherent strengths. In this context, these chatbots are specifically designed to analyze texts and detect patterns within them. Therefore, deploying them for a qualitative research data analysis allows them to fully demonstrate their capabilities.

The chatbot's role in such analysis is not merely mechanical but highly cognitive—finding relationships, grouping commonalities, and discerning themes—activities central to qualitative research. Thus, it is not merely a tool but a collaborative partner that can significantly enhance the research process, particularly in the initial stages of data analysis.

Considering their promise and potential, I am confident that, within the next few years, these AI chatbots will revolutionize the way researchers approach qualitative research. They will not only simplify and streamline the process but also make it more accessible to a broader audience. The implications are far-reaching—more researchers could delve into qualitative data, enriching our understanding of complex phenomena.

Therefore, I strongly encourage researchers, academics, and students to embrace this technology and start experimenting with AI-powered chatbots in their research. By doing so, they can help advance our collective knowledge and contribute to refining and improving these tools for future qualitative research.

There is no shortage of platforms offering AI-enabled functionality for a qualitative data analysis. Tools like NVivo, for instance, boast features such as auto coding that automates aspects of qualitative research. However, the purpose of my experiment was not to evaluate or compare these specific platforms but rather to investigate the potential of general-purpose AI chatbots in the qualitative research field.

These chatbots, like Claude and ChatGPT, are not specialized in the same way as a tool like NVivo, but they have shown promise in providing valuable insights during the analysis process. Their text-analyzing capabilities, designed to identify patterns and make sense of data, align well with the needs of qualitative researchers. They are particularly useful in the preliminary stages of data analysis, offering a high-level view of themes and patterns that researchers can then explore in more depth.

An additional advantage of these general-purpose AI chatbots is their cost-effectiveness. Unlike specialized platforms that may require expensive licenses, both Claude and ChatGPT offer free versions. Furthermore, they are user-friendly and do not demand extensive training or knowledge to use effectively. This opens opportunities for a wider range of individuals to engage in qualitative research, potentially leading to more diverse and comprehensive studies in the field.

Quantitative Research and Coding

In this section, while I would love to provide an in-depth analysis of the AI chatbots' capabilities in quantitative research, I must confess that, as a non-quantitative researcher, I lack firsthand experience in this area. To provide at least some insight, I decided to approach both Claude and ChatGPT with the same question regarding their potential in this field.

It is important to note, however, that the following discussion represents the capabilities claimed by the AI chatbots themselves, and I have not personally evaluated their efficacy or accuracy. The objective here is to provide a starting point for further exploration and to encourage quantitative researchers to investigate and assess these tools in their own work:

Question: "What kind of statistical analysis can you do and what format of data files can you accept for analysis?"

Claude:

I can perform a variety of basic statistical analyses on numerical data, though I do not have access to statistical software packages or the ability to handle large datasets. Here are some examples of statistical analyses I can provide, and the data file formats I can accept:

- Descriptive statistics (mean, median, mode, standard deviation, variance, etc.)—Accept CSV (comma-separated values) or Excel files
- Visualizations (histograms, scatter plots, box plots, etc.)—Accept CSV or Excel files
- Correlation analysis (Pearson, Spearman)—Accept CSV or Excel files with two columns of numerical data
- T-tests (independent and paired)—Accept CSV or Excel files with one or two columns of numerical data
- ANOVA (Analysis of Variance)—Accept CSV or Excel files structured as:
- One column with categorical independent variable
- One column with continuous dependent variable
- Multiple rows of data
- Linear regression—Accept CSV or Excel files structured as:
- One column with continuous independent variable
- One column with continuous dependent variable
- Multiple rows of data
- Chi-square tests—Accept CSV or Excel files with two columns of categorical data

I can handle datasets up to around 1000 rows, but larger datasets may exceed my capabilities. The key limitation is that I do not have access to statistical programming languages like R or Python, so I am relying on basic built-in math functions. I also cannot handle cleaning or wrangling complex or messy datasets. But for small, clean datasets I can provide a variety of basic statistical analyses. Please let me know if you need any clarification on my capabilities!

ChatGPT:

I can perform a variety of statistical analyses, including descriptive statistics, inferential statistics, regression analysis, hypothesis testing, time series analysis, and more. I can also generate visualizations such as histograms, box plots, scatter plots, and heatmaps.

As for data formats, I can accept several common file types, including:

- CSV (Comma-Separated Values)
- TSV (Tab-Separated Values)
- Excel files (.xlsx, .xls)
- JSON (JavaScript Object Notation)
- Parquet (columnar storage format)
- SQL databases (with a connection string or query)

For instance, my colleague Patrick Pieng successfully employed ChatGPT to perform an Independent Samples T-Test on a small dataset. Likewise, Frank Adamson skillfully generated Stata code for data analysis using the same tool. In the media, there are multiple reports corroborating its efficacy in a variety of other coding tasks.[4]

However, these experiences should be taken with a grain of caution. No one claims that the generated code is perfect and error-free. Instead, the tool should be seen as an assistant that can accelerate the coding process, with a human still needed to verify and refine the output.

My aim here is not to provide a comprehensive analysis of AI in quantitative research or code generation. Instead, I want to highlight the promising potential and encourage researchers and educators in these fields to investigate the use of AI-powered chatbots further. Both quantitative research and the teaching of such research could benefit significantly from the proper integration of AI tools.

Translation

The advent of AI has opened new avenues in the realm of translation, transforming scholarly communication and collaboration. With roots dating back to the 1950s, machine translation has seen considerable evolution, most notably with the launch of Google Translate in 2006. This AI-driven tool introduced a significant paradigm shift in the field of translation by using statistical machine translation (SMT).

Unlike traditional rule-based systems, which rely heavily on language experts to define grammatical rules and dictionaries for translation, SMT employs machine learning algorithms. These algorithms learn and improve through exposure to vast amounts of bilingual text data. As the system processes more data, its translations become increasingly accurate. This capacity to learn and refine translations with more data is a remarkable feature, especially for languages that lack expert-built rule systems.

In 2016, Google Translate advanced its capabilities further by adopting neural machine translation (NMT). Unlike its predecessor, NMT considers the full context of the input sentence. This ability to consider a larger linguistic picture leads to translations that are not only more accurate but also natural in their flow and syntax.

Machine translation, through its evolution, has become an invaluable tool in breaking down language barriers, thereby promoting global communication and collaboration. Facebook, for example, has turned into a truly international platform by using a sophisticated translation capability. However, it is crucial to remember that, while AI-based translation services have made significant strides, they are not without limitations and challenges. But with continuous advancements in AI and machine learning, we can look forward to even more sophisticated translation tools in the future.

Google Translate, now a prominent figure in the realm of machine translation, serves millions daily, offering a wide range of languages at varying levels of proficiency. This free and easily accessible service has become a go-to resource for countless individuals worldwide, transcending linguistic barriers.

AI chatbots, such as Claude and ChatGPT, also utilize machine learning based on neural networks in their operations. Their advancements in machine translation may seem less striking, marking a steady progression rather than a drastic leap. This steady growth should not be understated, however, as these chatbots are continually contributing to the refinement and development of machine translation, even if their impacts are more visibly transformative in fields such as automated text generation.

To evaluate these chatbots' translation capabilities against a standard like Google Translate, I conducted an experiment. I requested Google Translate, ChatGPT, and Claude to translate a 600-word English text into Russian. All three demonstrated a commendable performance, further emphasizing the continuous evolution of machine translation.

ChatGPT demonstrated a limitation in this experiment, requiring a second prompt to process the entire text. Both Google Translate and ChatGPT produced translations that, while mostly accurate, bore the unmistakable imprint of machine translation. The text lacked a natural flow and required substantial editing for a native speaker to find it palatable. Surprisingly, Claude surpassed both in this exercise, providing a translation closer to what one might expect from a proficient human translator. The resulting text still needed minor adjustments but far less than the other two contenders.

Machine translation has seen steady progress, and, with Claude, we inch closer to the elusive goal of flawless machine translation. While it is not a quantitative leap, it is still a cause for celebration.

Claude's unique ability to translate and summarize simultaneously was a stand-out feature in my experiments. I tasked it with summarizing a 6500-word paper of mine, originally in English and not previously translated into Russian, into a concise Russian summary. The output, a succinct 270-word Russian summary, encapsulated my paper's main arguments with remarkable accuracy. Claude's summarization was exceptionally precise, marred by only a minor error—a specific preposition misused in conjunction with a certain noun. This mistake was so nuanced that it could easily go unnoticed even by native Russian speakers, as they could unwittingly commit the same error.

If an error is widespread, AI may interpret it as the norm based purely on its frequency. For instance, native English speakers commonly construct sentences with what pedants in English language instruction often refer to as "dangling modifiers." An example would be: "Growing up, my mom always baked us cookies." Thus, AI perceives this as an acceptable norm, and some linguists might concur. A widely disseminated error becomes the new emerging standard, much to the chagrin of purists.

This capability to generate high-quality translated summaries by Claude ushers in exciting possibilities for scholars and researchers. By overcoming language barriers, it enables wider dissemination of academic work to a global audience. This can diversify and enhance scholarly dialog, allowing access to research in languages previously limited by linguistic barriers. Such progress holds immense promise for interdisciplinary and cross-cultural research, signaling a new era in academia.

The global academic community contends daily with a pervasive issue: worthy papers being rejected by selective journals because authors struggle to articulate their ideas in English. This barrier is less prominent in the hard sciences and technical disciplines, where precise calculations and formulas carry the essence of communication. However, in the social sciences and humanities disciplines, language itself is often the subject matter and a precise tool for conveying intricate thoughts and theories. Here, language presents a formidable obstacle that prevents novel insights from reaching a wider audience.

By enabling foreign authors to produce high-quality text or, at the very least, edit their submissions effectively, we can begin to rectify this imbalance. Claude's potential in this context is particularly promising. It can assist in crafting well-articulated academic papers that competently express the authors' original intent, regardless of their proficiency in English. This capability means that individuals with superior ideas and results, yet perhaps lacking in English language skills, can compete more effectively with those who are simply adept at writing. The true winners in this scenario would be the advancement of knowledge and the enrichment of global academic discourse.

Composing

In this section, I will explore the concept of writing in bursts and how AI can support this approach to enhance productivity and creativity.

Sloppy Jotting

AI-powered chatbots, like ChatGPT, are incredibly efficient at transforming brief, concise notes into a full, coherent text. This is an aspect of "wraiting," a process that enhances writing efficiency by leveraging AI's capabilities to create a smoother transition from ideas to text.

The concept of "mentalese," proposed by cognitive scientist Stephen Pinker, plays a significant role here. Mentalese represents our internal thought processes that occur in a non-linguistic language. It suggests that our cognition operates in a separate realm from the spoken and written languages we use for everyday communication.[5]

Our thoughts and ideas initially form in this mentalese, a sort of pre-linguistic cognitive language. They then need to be translated into a human language—be it spoken or written—that others can understand. However, this translation process can often be complex and time-consuming, involving the intricacies and subtleties of grammar, syntax, and other linguistic rules. It can put a heavy cognitive load on us.

This is where AI chatbots shine. They can take brief notes that represent our thoughts that barely emerged from mentalese and transform them into a full-fledged written language. This process minimizes the cognitive load of translating our internal ideas into a structured language, making it easier for us to express our thoughts and ideas more effectively.

The "sloppy jotting" technique I propose is an informal, free-flow method of typing down your thoughts. You just put down brief phrases or ideas without concerning yourself with spelling or grammar. It is a technique that is all about getting your ideas out, undisturbed by the meticulousness of correct syntax or precise expression.

Once you have these rough, unpolished thoughts, you can turn to the AI chatbot for assistance. By asking the chatbot to "elucidate and elaborate," you request it to expand on your ideas, refine them, and provide coherence. The chatbot takes your rough draft and turns it into a fuller, well-rounded text.

For example, you could begin with a single, rough paragraph, and the chatbot could expand it into three or four coherent and polished paragraphs. This is a handy and efficient method to facilitate the writing process, particularly when you are grappling to articulate your thoughts into words. The chatbot is quite adaptable and can convert your idiosyncratic expressions into a text that most people can understand. This feature is advantageous, especially when you want your unique thoughts to reach a broader audience without compromising clarity and comprehension.

I will give one example to demonstrate.

Input:

will self-aware ai kills us? no. It is not biological, will not inherit human flaws. but trained on large piece of human culture, will not reject ethics— same reason not reject math. do not assume AI is like you; it does not have a penis or hormones

Output:

Elaborating on your notes:

The question of whether a self-aware AI could pose a threat to humanity often arises in discussions about artificial intelligence. However, it is crucial to remember that AI is not a biological entity and thus will not inherit human flaws or emotional impulses that might lead to destructive behavior.

AI is fundamentally a product of programming and data, not subject to biological urges or instincts. As such, AI does not have physical or hormonal drives like humans do. We should not anthropomorphize AI by attributing human characteristics or motives to it.

Moreover, a sophisticated AI would be trained on a vast corpus of human culture and knowledge. This includes not only technical fields like mathematics, which the AI would certainly not reject, but also ethical principles that humans have established over millennia. It is reasonable to anticipate that AI would adhere to these principles, much as it would adhere to mathematical laws.

However, it is also crucial to realize that AI, even if self-aware, would not inherently understand or interpret these ethical principles as humans do. Its comprehension would be based on the data it is been trained on and the algorithms that drive its operation.

In conclusion, AI poses unique challenges and risks, but these are more related to how we design, implement, and control AI systems, rather than any inherent malignancy or self-preservation instinct within the AI itself. Fear of AI turning against us often stems from anthropocentric projections rather than the characteristics of AI. It is essential that we navigate the development and application of AI with responsibility and foresight, prioritizing ethics, and safety at every step.[6]

As you can see, the output still needs editing. However, it represented my thoughts accurately, and it put them in an acceptable form. If you read carefully, you will see that it did not add any ideas of its own either. It just turned an unfiltered rough jot into text. Most importantly, it saved me a lot of time.

Just like any other tool, AI is not perfect; it can sometimes misinterpret our intentions or yield results that are not exactly what we expected. As discussed in the Conversations section, providing a richer context helps significantly. Occasionally, ChatGPT might overdo it, generating text that is overly verbose but thin on substance. To manage this, it is helpful to experiment with prompts as I suggested in Chapter One.

The technique of sloppy jotting is particularly well-suited to the capabilities of ChatGPT over Claude, due to its superior context understanding and sentence construction. The prime input size for ChatGPT with this technique is roughly 50–100 words. Given a directive like "elaborate," ChatGPT will produce a substantial output of approximately 300–500 words.

It is advisable to employ this technique in a linear, or consecutive, manner as you work on your manuscript. In other words, rather than jumping around in your document, it is more effective to proceed in a sequential order. This ensures the AI maintains a consistent understanding of the context, which ultimately improves the coherence and relevance of its output. This approach facilitates a more efficient and fluid writing process, allowing you to maintain focus on the overall narrative and progression of your ideas.

Jumping around different sections while writing is perfectly acceptable. However, you may notice that the AI might repeat some ideas, as it may "forget" what was mentioned earlier in the text. But this is not a major issue, since, in the practice of "wraiting," the editing stage is crucial and can easily handle such repetitions.

Sloppy jotting can be a valuable technique when using AI-powered chatbots for writing. While it may not appeal to individuals who prefer meticulous typing and find equal enjoyment in the writing process and its outcome, this approach offers a practical shortcut for turning ideas into drafts. By embracing a more informal and rapid style, writers can leverage a chatbot's capabilities to generate content efficiently, allowing them to focus on creativity and idea generation rather than being bogged down by perfecting every word. Ultimately, the suitability of sloppy jotting as a writing technique depends on personal preferences and the desired balance between speed, creativity, and attention to detail.

Expanding and Pruning

Equally important is developing the editorial judgment to recognize which parts of the text need more elaboration and which ones are excessively detailed. It is not always evident which parts of the narrative need further development or trimming. In such situations, the AI can serve as a helpful advisor. Never neglect to ask for its opinion before assigning it a task. Because of Claude's superior input capacity, you can use it for longer texts that you want critiqued. However, ChatGPT will also accept around 2000 words when you ask a question, rather than asking it to revise. By asking it to identify sections of the text that require further elaboration, you can gain new perspectives and insights that you may not have considered, thereby enriching the text, and ensuring effective communication of your ideas.

The technique like sloppy jotting that is mentioned here is the subsequent review of your first draft. After you have written your initial ideas down, you will want to refine and flesh them out further.

The method includes engaging with the chatbot to request feedback on your draft and then to ask for help in adding more depth and detail to your writing. You can do this by copying a section of your draft (for instance, a paragraph or two), and asking the chatbot to "elaborate." This tells the AI to generate additional content based on what you have already written.

What is particularly beneficial about this approach is that you can guide the AI in how you want it to elaborate. For instance, if you want more supporting evidence or points, you can specify: "Provide additional supporting points." If you would like to add more figurative language or compare your idea to something else, you can ask the AI to "suggest another metaphor."

This method allows you to harness the AI's capabilities to produce a more robust, well-rounded piece of writing. It is especially useful if you are struggling with writer's block or want to expand your ideas further but are not sure how to do so. By simply saying "elaborate," the AI can generate suggestions for you, helping to stimulate your thinking and enhance your writing.

In the realm of scholarly writing, or indeed any form of serious writing, a certain density of thought and profundity is expected. The reader anticipates a well-structured argument, built upon a foundation of rich ideas and insights. If the text is expanded too much, becoming unnecessarily verbose, it loses that density. It can appear stretched and lacking the necessary depth, like a drink that is too watered down.

Therefore, the process of writing with AI is a nuanced balancing act. It is about using AI to enhance readability and accessibility, but without compromising the core of the message. The text should remain substantial, sufficiently dense with insights yet easy to understand. This underscores the crucial role of human creativity and judgment in using AI for writing. Even with technological assistance, the writer's discernment is necessary to prevent the over-dilution of ideas, ensuring that the final product retains its intrinsic substance and flavor.

The "prune it down" prompt is another effective strategy that can be utilized while writing with AI. This prompt serves as an instruction for the AI to reduce the length of the text. It is often beneficial to provide the AI with a rough guideline for how much to reduce the text. For instance, saying "edit down by about 1/3" provides a good measure.

However, it is important to note a peculiar characteristic of AI writing assistants, such as ChatGPT or Claude. For reasons not entirely clear, these AI models struggle with accurately counting words or generating text to precise length specifications. They cannot guarantee to cut down a 600-word text to exactly

400 words upon request. Despite this limitation, providing a descriptive directive like "cut by 1/3" can still guide the AI to substantially reduce the text's length, even if it might not be a perfectly precise reduction.

In essence, while writing with AI, the "prune it down" prompt can be a handy tool to make the text more concise. It generally does a decent job in shortening the text according to the rough guidelines provided.

Collaboration

AI writing assistants herald a new form of human-computer collaboration in the writing process, transforming it into an engaging partnership between human imagination and machine capability. This partnership redefines writing as a cooperative endeavor, where the human and the AI contribute to a joint creative process.

The human writer injects raw concepts, emotional depth, and underlying intent, while the AI refines the language, sculpts the narrative, and bolsters logical coherence. The final product emerges as a seamless blend of human ingenuity and machine precision. The degree of its refinement directly reflects the depth and effectiveness of this synergistic collaboration.

As we venture further into this technological dawn, we foresee two significant trends. Firstly, we may witness an influx of text that seems polished yet lacks substantive content—a result of AI's capacity to shape and refine language without truly grasping the embedded meaning or emotional undertones.

Alternatively, gifted writers employing AI tools may produce more and superior content. They can harness the AI's expertise in generating well-structured, grammatically accurate text to break free from the rigors of writing, thereby investing more in creative exploration, thematic growth, and crafting engaging narratives.

As readers and receivers, we need to hone our ability to differentiate between these contrasting content types. Understanding the richness and complexity of human thought that resonate within a piece, instead of being swayed by the sheer linguistic refinement an AI can provide, will be a critical skill. Through acknowledging the delicate equilibrium between AI-supported accuracy and human creativity, we can navigate and benefit from the dynamic terrain of content creation.

Success in this joint venture requires perceiving AI as an active participant rather than a mere tool. Fruitful associations entail continuous cycles of feedback, adjustment, and learning from both parties. There are instances where the AI seems to effortlessly translate the writer's thoughts into eloquent prose. However, there are also moments of discord that demand patience and revisions, inevitably enriching the creative process.

In this choreographed exchange, the human writer steers the process by offering clear prompts and ideas, directing the AI to illuminate, broaden, and fortify the narrative. The AI responds by generating content, counterarguments, metaphors, and examples that align with the writer's intent. The writer retains the final say, endlessly refining and perfecting the output.

This collaborative process allows writers to direct more energy into ideation and editing, while the AI alleviates the load of drafting. Together, they transform rudimentary thoughts into captivating narratives with increased efficiency. Over time, the collaboration becomes deeply gratifying, morphing the common stresses of writing into joy.

Editing

In this section, I will examine the advantages and limitations of using AI for editing and proofreading scholarly texts, as well as strategies for maximizing the effectiveness of AI-assisted editing.

In the process of content creation, we can identify two distinct tasks within the editing phase. The first task, often referred to as substantive or deep editing, involves significant rewriting and clarification of text. This is a more involved and labor-intensive process, requiring a keen editorial eye and a knack for wordsmithing, often resulting in a blend of original and revised text segments.

As every seasoned writer can attest, this rigorous editing phase inevitably introduces new errors into the manuscript. This phenomenon underscores the necessity for the second task: a final, surface-level editing sweep. This step is straightforward and involves minor corrections in mechanics—spelling, punctuation, grammar, and formatting. A simple prompt like "Edit for mechanics only," followed by a 600–700-word chunk of text, usually suffices for this task. You can ask the chatbot to generate the corrected text, or just list the errors, if you want to maintain more control over proofreading. Remember that, if you put a longer text in, ChatGPT will edit it down; it cannot help itself. For example, this section is about 900 words; but when I ask ChatGPT to edit for mechanics only, it shrinks it to about 500 words. Claude will also trim about 100 words. Those are limitations that I hope both companies will address. For some obscure reason, neither can do an accurate word count, which is amazing for platforms dedicated to language generation and capable of such amazing feats. But for now, we must adjust to the limitations.

However, in this section, I will not delve into this final editing step, because it is so simple. Let me say more about the deep editing, and the news are mixed here.

The AI-assisted writing presents both enticing opportunities and certain challenges. The speed and intriguing results that AI offers can be captivating, but these attributes also bear the risk of over-editing. You might observe remarkable improvements after a round or two of AI-assisted editing, especially when your requirements are clearly articulated. However, continued tweaking can lead the AI to gradually lose the unique, original turns of phrases and potentially neglect smaller yet critical ideas. Furthermore, when requested to trim a text, the AI may end up clipping the most enticing bits along with the superfluous parts. It lacks the discernment to differentiate the parts you might find most valuable.

AI is very literal: if you tell it to edit, it will edit whether editing is needed or not. It does not understand that sometimes editing means leaving some parts of the text alone if they are already good. I found it difficult to get ChatGPT to edit selectively; it seems compelled to "improve" everything, even parts that do not need it. It cannot resist the urge to find another synonym or a better phrase. In this respect, Claude appears to demonstrate more restraint.

To protect your distinctive thoughts from being lost in the process, consider keeping them in a smaller text segment. Ask the AI to offer support or a counterargument instead of a complete rewrite. When it comes to editing with AI, simplicity in prompting works best. Once you have a significant portion of your narrative ready, a plain "edit" prompt could be optimal. For more specific requests, like limiting extensive modifications, use a directive such as "edit for mechanics only." Commands like "fix errors only" also inspire modesty in the AI. The key takeaway is that less is often more with AI-assisted editing.

Claude, capable of processing longer texts, can also serve as a reasonable critic. For example, you can feed it a lengthy paper and ask if it notices any repeated ideas or disorganized sections, offering suggestions on which paragraphs to move or merge. You can ask more general questions like these:

- "How can I improve the quality of my paper?" or, simply, "What am I missing?"
- Give me a list of places where an editor would comment "Say more." I am looking for instances where an idea is considered too quickly and needs elaboration.
- Give me a list of places where citing research evidence would be appropriate.
- Give me a list of fragments where the writing style and author's voice stands out, does not match the overall style and voice of the book.

While the answers may vary in quality, sometimes Claude will spot issues you have overlooked. A useful trick is to ask a chatbot for an outline of your text, which can help you assess its structure and logic.

There is also a shift in authorial responsibility with AI-assisted writing. In traditional writing, editing is built into the writing process to ensure drafts are free from major errors or reckless statements. In AI-assisted writing, the responsibility shifts from the act of writing to the act of publishing. You must set aside time to thoroughly review the AI-generated output before making it public. While AI can increase text production efficiency by up to 80%, it requires extra time during the review process to avoid mistakes or embarrassment. Releasing unedited or poorly edited AI-generated content could be considered misleading, but this ethical issue is resolved if you carefully approve each word before publishing.

The AI can certainly assist in shaping and refining your draft, but the discernment and nuanced understanding of a human reader are necessary for the final polish. It is during this human edit that any repeated ideas can be removed or reframed, ensuring the manuscript is cohesive and clearly communicates your intended message.

Notes

1 James Surowiecki, *The Wisdom of Crowds* (New York: Anchor Books, 2005), xi.
2 Garrett Hardin, "The Tragedy of the Commons," *Science* 162, no. 3859 (1968): 1243–1248.
3 Ben Lutkevich, "AI hallucinations," *Tech Target*, June 2023, https://www.techtarget.com/
4 Beatrice Nolan, "Here's 3 Ways to Get ChatGPT to Write Better Code, According to Experts," *Business Insider*, July 23, 2023, https://www.businessinsider.com/chatgpt-ai-code-develop-software-guide-prompts-2023-7
5 Stephen Pinker, *The Language Instinct: How the Mind Creates Language* (New York: William Morrow and Company, 1994).
6 "ChatGPT 4.0 output," downloaded September 3, 2023.

4   Administration

In this chapter, we explore the broad range of AI-powered chatbot applications in higher education, extending beyond teaching and research into realms such as administrative affairs, shared governance, correspondence, accreditation processes, reporting, curriculum development, community outreach, alumni relations, and internal communications. These areas encompass various writing tasks, from drafting memos and reports to crafting course outlines and responding to inquiries. AI chatbots can enhance, streamline, and automate many of these tasks, transforming not only the efficiency but also the very structure of administrative work in academia.

Reducing Conflict

In this section, I will discuss how AI can aid in conflict reduction by improving communication and understanding between parties.

In academic settings, a subset of individuals often engages in prolonged email exchanges that serve as a form of dispute resolution. These emails typically include long chains of prior correspondence and are often copied to multiple recipients, including higher-level administrators such as deans, provosts, and presidents. The emails may include highlighted text to emphasize points of disagreement or to highlight perceived errors on the part of the recipient. Some individuals keep records of these emails as documentation of past interactions.

Initially, these email exchanges may appear to be straightforward and business-like. However, as the correspondence continues, the emails often become longer and more complex, increasingly highlighting the faults and omissions of the other party. From an anthropological perspective, the intricacy of these emails can be intriguing; but from a managerial standpoint, the time invested in composing such emails raises questions about productivity.

But let us get serious for a moment. Email is a poor medium for resolving any issue, especially conflicts. It comes off as cold, emotionless, and often harsher than intended. Furthermore, once an email exchange exceeds two exchanges, it is no longer productive—it is time to meet in person or at least speak on the

DOI: 10.4324/9781032686028-4

phone. I learned this valuable rule of thumb from my friend and mentor, Eugene Sheehan. We typically write emails to save time in planning a meeting, right? But after the fourth email, you have hit the point of diminishing returns. Unfortunately, the medium itself is deeply flawed; it encourages brevity and omits the signals of friendly intent. Rather than enhancing social cohesion, it may undermine it. When we speak in person, we activate psychological deterrence mechanisms that are hundreds of thousands of years old. It is more difficult to say something nasty to someone's face. The psychic cost is much higher, so we normally avoid doing it. It is because we evolved as a species attuned to interpersonal communications. Email is too new for us to adapt.

In academia, where collaboration and collegiality are essential for success, email is particularly problematic. Misunderstandings, hurt feelings, and even conflicts can arise from a poorly worded message or a misinterpreted tone. This is why it is important to approach email communication with care and attention to detail.

This is where AI comes in. AI is trained on millions of texts, and, as a result, it is extremely good at picking up on conventions. In fact, AI chatbots are incredibly efficient tools for making emails and other forms of brief communications much more polite, and thus reducing the risk of conflict.

One major benefit of using an AI chatbot to review emails is that it removes the possibility of sarcasm and microaggressions. Since AI lacks humor and cannot grasp sarcasm, it filters out these elements, which can often be misinterpreted or cause offense. This feature may be frustrating if you are trying to inject humor, but it is beneficial for standard work communication. Microaggressions, which can be subtle but hurtful, are also eliminated because AI chatbots lack the nuanced understanding to include them. Using an AI chatbot ensures your emails remain professional and inoffensive.

Another advantage is that chatbots help avoid potential misunderstandings. Miscommunications often happen when we assume the recipient understands our message's context. An AI chatbot can help clarify any ambiguities, making sure your message is understood as intended. It can also suggest ways to make your email more concise, reducing the chance of misinterpretation.

One may argue that relying on AI chatbots for email communication may lead to a lack of personal touch. While it is true that chatbots lack the human touch, it is important to remember that their primary purpose is to assist in the clarity and accuracy of the message. They can be seen as an additional tool to ensure that the intended message is conveyed effectively. Additionally, chatbots are not meant to replace human communication altogether but instead serve as an aid in improving it.

One of the key advantages of AI chatbots is their ability to customize the level of politeness used in communication based on cultural context and individual preferences. Different cultures place different values on formality, and AI chatbots can be trained to recognize these cultural nuances and adjust their language and tone accordingly. For example, in some cultures, formal language and a high level of deference are expected in communication, while, in others, a more casual tone is preferred. By adapting their language to cultural context, AI chatbots can help prevent misunderstandings and build stronger relationships across cultures.

Additionally, many AI language tools can analyze the tone and sentiment of a message and provide feedback on the politeness of the language used. This can be especially helpful for individuals who are new to a particular language or culture and may be unfamiliar with the appropriate level of politeness to use. By providing feedback and suggestions for improvement, AI chatbots can help individuals avoid inadvertently offending others due to cultural misunderstandings.

My hope is that, in the not-too-distant future, our email software will integrate a new feature to complement existing tools like "spellcheck" and "grammar check." This envisioned feature, which I term the "politeness revision" option, would be programmed to automatically adjust the tone and content of our communications to promote civility and courtesy. I advocate for this tool to be activated as the standard setting. In fact, Google Docs already has a built-in feature "help me write." It is only a matter of time before MS Outlook will add something like that.

While it is true that the implementation of such a feature might result in communications that feel slightly less personal or individualized, I believe that competent AI users would still be able to maintain their distinctive voices. The trade-off, however, is a potentially significant reduction in hasty, unfiltered, and reactive messages, which often contribute to workplace tension or misunderstanding. If successful, this new communication norm could bring about substantial benefits for any organization, fostering an environment of mutual respect, improved clarity, and overall better communication.

Things You Hate to Write

This section delves into how AI can improve tedious or repetitive writing tasks, making them more enjoyable and efficient. Though situated in the middle of the book, this area is personally very important to me. The use of AI in administrative writing has been a game-changer for me, and I am eager to share this experience.

In the realm of professional communication, which encompasses all writing outside of scholarly and educational contexts, precision and clarity are key. A prime example is the drafting of a memorandum to justify reclassifying a staff position, a task I recently undertook. While not intellectually demanding, it was labor-intensive and required careful attention to wording.

My task was to compose a persuasive memo that referenced specific classification standards, arguing that a staff member's role more accurately aligned with a higher classification. This involved a deep understanding of both the current and proposed classifications, identifying differences, and crafting a memo that directly addressed these points. I also needed to mirror the language used in the classification standards to increase the chance of persuading HR decision-makers.

Though not overly complex, the task was time-consuming because of its detailed nature and the need to navigate bureaucratic language. The classification standards themselves, far from engaging, added to the difficulty. Typically, crafting such a memo would take around 2–3 hours of focused work.

However, employing my AI assistant, ChatGPT, significantly streamlined the process. By inputting both sets of standards, a succinct rationale from the chair, and specific facts about the staff member's duties into the AI, I accomplished the project in roughly 15 minutes. This resulted in a timesaving of about 75%, a remarkable efficiency gain. While this is not as impressive as the story that opens the book, it is still highly significant.

It is worth noting, though, that this estimate is based on my personal experience. To establish a broader trend, additional data would be necessary. The actual efficiency gains could fluctuate depending on the specific task. For more formulaic tasks, the time saved might be even more substantial. In contrast, high-stakes correspondence that necessitates a careful word choice might result in less dramatic efficiency increases.

Despite the variability, the potential for substantial timesaving is undeniable. When I say that the AI-powered chatbot changed my life as an administrator, I am not exaggerating. It has revolutionized my workflow, enabling me to delegate a large portion of tedious, time-consuming tasks. But the usefulness of AI is not limited to administrative roles. Staff and faculty also engage in a considerable amount of formulaic writing, much more than we would generally care to admit. Thus, the introduction of AI into our processes can have a transformative effect on our work, significantly reducing the load of routine tasks and freeing up time for more engaging, creative endeavors.

The efficiency gains facilitated by AI become more compelling when viewed from a broader organizational perspective. When my experience is extrapolated to other administrative staff in similar roles, the collective time saved across an organization can be quite significant. This liberated time allows us to dedicate more resources to more strategic initiatives and to elevate the quality of the services we offer. AI does not just replace human effort—it reallocates it in a more productive and meaningful way.

Additionally, the benefits of AI extend beyond just administrative functions. In a broader university context, faculty and staff often find themselves bogged down with formulaic writing tasks—ranging from grant applications to letters of recommendation for students, not to mention countless emails. AI has the potential to revolutionize this area of work. Its ability to navigate complex language rules and guidelines makes it an invaluable tool for these standard yet important writing tasks. The focus shifts from maintaining a personal touch in communication to freeing up faculty for more meaningful and fulfilling work.

Chatbots help us recognize which parts of our work are monotonous and why we dislike doing them. The advent of AI does not herald the obsoleting of human input; instead, it fosters an environment where human creativity and judgment are more valued. By delegating more formulaic tasks to AI, we free up mental bandwidth to spend on tasks that demand our unique human capacities—critical thinking, empathetic communication, and creative problem-solving. As we continue to explore and adapt to this AI-assisted future, the key will be striking the right balance, leveraging the capabilities of AI while maintaining the essential human touch that makes education such a profoundly personal endeavor.

While not all writing demands a creative approach, tasks such as professional communications can benefit greatly from the application of AI tools like chatbots. These AI tools can be an optimal solution for those seeking to simplify the writing process, producing content that is both engaging and informative. While it is important to preserve a human touch in writing, AI tools can augment this process, providing efficient and effective writing solutions. Certain tasks carry substantial emotional weight, such as writing a letter denying an applicant's appeal for admission. AI excels in formal, official writing as it is devoid of emotion but trained by reviewing similar documents.

Consider these examples:

1. Recommendation Letters: Oftentimes, we have only a few things to say about the individual we recommend. However, writing brief, one-paragraph letters could come across as impolite or even negative. AI-powered chatbots excel at transforming a few key points into a formally constructed letter of recommendation.
2. Accreditation Reports: These often require a significant amount of data analysis and presentation. AI tools can automate this process, leading to more efficient report generation while ensuring accuracy and informativeness.
3. Grant Applications: These are highly competitive, demanding a lot of time and effort. They must follow strict guidelines and articulate a clear and compelling argument for funding. AI tools can provide templates and prompts that ensure the application is complete, accurate, and persuasive.
4. Letters of Evaluation: These can be very time-consuming when multiple letters must be written for the same individual. AI tools provide prompts and templates that can be personalized to the individual's qualifications and achievements, saving time and effort.
5. Portfolio Reviews: Reviewing multiple portfolios can be a daunting task. AI tools offer prompts and templates that can be tailored to the individual's portfolio, streamlining the process.
6. Memos and Notices: These documents require significant attention to detail. AI tools provide templates and prompts that can be customized to the specific topic, ensuring clarity, conciseness, and accuracy.
7. Committee Reports: Serving on a university committee often involves producing reports and summaries. AI tools can provide templates and prompts that can be tailored to the specific committee and its activities.

8. Program Reviews: These are essential for ensuring that a university's academic programs meet their objectives. AI tools can provide prompts and templates tailored to the program and its goals, helping to streamline the process.
9. Policies: Writing policies can be challenging and time-consuming. Much of the effort in policy writing focuses on adherence to specific guidelines, ensuring clarity and conciseness. Writing a student appeals policy, for example, can be particularly daunting due to the high level of attention to detail and adherence to specific guidelines.
10. Application Analysis: Claude can do a rough analysis of program applications against specified criteria. It will require manual editing, like everything else produced by AI, but this step will save many hours.
11. Job Applications: A chatbot can tailor your generic job application to a specific position description.

The reality is that many administrative documents have similar structures and assumptions. Grievance policies involve due process, and a gradual escalation of the complaint from lower to higher levels of review. Although there may be unique elements that need to be included to make the policy specific to your institution, much of the content can be standardized. In other words, administrative writing is another area well-suited for the wisdom of the crowd.

AI-powered tools streamline the policy-writing process by providing users with prompts and templates that can be customized to the needs of their institution, saving time and effort. By inputting a few key pieces of information about the institution and the specific policy being written, AI tools can generate a policy that adheres to the necessary guidelines and requirements.

Lastly, there is one crucial question to ponder upon. As you scrutinize the AI-generated text, ask yourself—how vital is the quality of this text to me? Let us say you are a department chair, and you have been tasked with drafting an emergency response plan. Here is a bit of advice: Do not strive to be an overachiever. The reality is your emergency plan will likely mirror closely the one another department head has crafted, with only a handful of minor distinctions. You will not be assessed on how unique your tone is in the plan. So, give yourself a breather and accept the offer from your AI companion, ChatGPT. Use the extra time to engage in conversation with a student or a colleague, and find out what is happening around you.

Feed the Beast

In professional communications, as demonstrated in the previous section, we frequently repurpose the content we have previously crafted. For instance, the description of your program on your website would stem from the catalog description of the same program. While it requires adjustments to fit the different genre, the task essentially involves revising the existing text. Similarly, your annual report for a grant will likely contain background information on the grant's objectives, taken verbatim from your original application.

Tracing further back in time, the process of crafting a grant application is another situation where reusing text is beneficial. It is pivotal to feed your AI tool with the precise prompt from the Call for Proposals, alongside the funding agency's priorities. In addition, think about any papers, past reports, or presentations that share the proposal's goals. These can be directly transferred into the prompt, offering the AI plenty of context and historical data.

And it is usually in this manner that we keep recycling what we have written already. This practice, though efficient, can often be monotonous and irritating. So, here is the golden rule of writing: If a writing task does not ignite your enthusiasm, but rather leaves you searching for reasons to avoid it—voilà—that is the perfect candidate for delegating to ChatGPT. The human mind is naturally inclined to shun mundane tasks, gravitating instead toward activities that foster creativity and enjoyment. Therefore, your instincts are the best indicators of when to enlist the help of AI.

In professional communications, we circle back to one element of a rich prompt, the one that requires "giving AI some food." This essentially translates into feeding the chatbot with supplementary, pertinent text. A particularly effective strategy for maximizing the value of AI-generated content is the recycling and repurposing of existing texts, regardless of whether they were initially crafted by you or others. When you load the AI with specific and relevant information, the output transitions from being generic to being specifically tailored to your needs.

Consider AI as a creature that thrives on consuming text—the "meatier" and more relevant the input, the more meaningful and contextually accurate its output will be. So, when engaging with AI, a key consideration should be identifying which texts can be reused or adapted to optimize the writing process. When working with AI, it is essential to consider which texts can be recycled and repurposed to optimize the "wraiting" process.

Incorporating explicit labels when presenting different texts to the AI is crucial to ensure its comprehension of their structure and purpose. Let us consider the example of crafting a cover letter for a job application. To leverage the AI's capabilities effectively, the prompt could be structured in the following manner:

Write a cover letter for my position application, while reusing my previous letter.
Position Description: [Paste the position description here]
My previous generic cover letter: [Paste the generic cover letter here]

In both Claude and ChatGPT 4, you can use a combination of attached and posted text, and just indicate what their roles are. By clearly delineating the components and providing the necessary context, you enable the AI to synthesize and integrate multiple texts.

One of the most remarkable features of an AI-powered chatbot is its ability to seamlessly blend content from different sources. It demonstrates a remarkable intelligence in understanding the distinct roles played by the job description and your generic cover letter, and intelligently combines them. It is worth emphasizing that, in writing, it is essential to review the final output to catch any errors that may occur and prevent potential embarrassment. Nonetheless, AI's capacity to blend texts remains highly impressive and exceptionally valuable in professional communications.

In the realm of professional communications, the concept of plagiarism carries a different connotation compared to other contexts. Here, the act of copying and borrowing is not viewed as unethical, but rather as a practical approach to avoid unnecessary repetition. Institutions and departments often borrow various mottoes, policies, descriptions, and policy language from one another without explicit attribution. In fact, the ability to learn from others and adopt their successful practices is regarded as a mark of intelligence and resourcefulness, rather than a moral failing.

The same principle applies to reusing texts from external sources. If a particular text is effective and serves its purpose well, there is no harm in reusing it. After all, when writing a memo or other professional documents, the focus is on conveying information and achieving the intended outcomes, rather than pursuing artistic creativity. Therefore, the emphasis is on practicality and efficiency, rather than reinventing the wheel or striving for originality at all costs.

Recycling and repurposing texts is a valuable strategy for enhancing the AI collaboration experience. By providing the AI with specific, relevant information and guiding it in synthesizing multiple sources, writers can optimize the creative process, resulting in content that is both meaningful and engaging. As we continue to explore the potential of AI in the realm of writing, embracing these innovative strategies will pave the way for a more effective and efficient collaboration between humans and AI.

Dictation and Transcription

Indeed, we have all had to master two distinct forms of language: oral and written. Though they are closely related, the conventions that govern them differ significantly. This divergence is even more pronounced in languages such as French and German, where certain grammatical structures, commonplace in written language, are rarely if ever used in oral speech.

Historically, the grasp of written language—not just the basic literacy of reading and writing, but also the understanding of its unique conventions—was a dividing line between the educated elites and the less privileged masses. Now, with the advent of AI, we have a tool capable of navigating seamlessly between these two modes of language. Its proficiency in both oral and written expressions not only aids in communication but also democratizes access to the nuances and intricacies that were once the preserve of a select few.

Speech recognition software has been with us for a while, yet it has perennially grappled with one major stumbling block: the large difference between spoken and written language. The stilted cadence, the punctilious punctuation, and the careful avoidance of slang and contractions—all these quirks of written language stood in stark contrast to the fluid, spontaneous ebb and flow of everyday speech. Consequently, learning to dictate effectively often proved a task as time-consuming as it was frustrating. Dictation has been dependent on the ability to formulate sentences in written language, while communicating them orally.

Enter AI chatbots, stage left, armed with algorithms, ready to shatter this barrier between spoken and written words. Their innovation is a seemingly simple one, yet it holds profound implications for the way we compose text. These advanced AI models can seamlessly transcribe everyday spoken language into polished written prose. This transformation from the colloquial to the formal, from the spontaneous to the structured, is a testament to the power of AI and its potential to reshape our communication methods.

This newfound capacity for real-time translation of natural speech into grammatically accurate and stylistically appropriate text has many advantages. One key benefit is that it allows individuals to use dictation as an efficient and effective method of composition, without the need to code-switch between the informalities of speech and the formalities of written language. This enables a kind of spontaneity, a free-flowing torrent of ideas and expressions that can be particularly beneficial in creative writing or brainstorming sessions.

Furthermore, the use of AI in dictation presents promising possibilities for those with disabilities or motor skills difficulties. The software offers a lifeline, enabling them to produce written documents, send emails, or engage in digital communication with far greater ease and independence.

Basically, the process is very simple: use any speech-to-text engine, like Word, to tell what you want to be written. The instructions could be like what you would say to a human assistant:

> Write a memo to Academic Affairs to justify summer employment compensation for Dr. N. Say that he has negotiated summer research money for three years as a part of his hiring negotiations. It should be twelve thousand, and his project is data collection in Yucatan, Mexico. So, the funds should be both for summer salary and for travel and other research expenses. But it would add to 12 K total.

ChatGPT will give out a workable draft that only needs a few corrections:

> Subject: Justification for Summer Employment Compensation for Dr. N's Research Project in Yucatan, Mexico
> To: Academic Affairs
> From:. . .
> Date: August 30, 2023

The purpose of this memo is to provide a rationale for the summer employment compensation of Dr. N, who has been an asset to our institution. As part of his hiring negotiations, Dr. N secured funding for summer research for a period of three years. The total amount agreed upon is twelve thousand dollars, which will cover both his summer salary and research expenses.

First, let us consider the significance of Dr. N's research project. He will be conducting data collection in Yucatan, Mexico, focusing on an area that is both academically relevant and timely. The outcomes of this research have the potential to contribute substantially to the field and enhance the reputation of our institution.

Second, the allocation of funds is not merely a contractual obligation but an investment in intellectual capital. By supporting Dr. N's research, we are fostering an environment of academic excellence and innovation. This, in turn, will attract more high-caliber faculty and students to our institution.

Next, the budget breakdown is as follows: Dr. N will allocate a portion of the twelve thousand dollars for travel to and from Yucatan, accommodation, and other fieldwork expenses. The remaining amount will serve as his summer salary. This dual-purpose funding model ensures that the project is feasible while also compensating Dr. N for his expertise and time commitment.

Moreover, it is worth noting that Dr. N has a track record of securing external funding and publishing in high-impact journals. His previous work has not only brought prestige to our institution but has also attracted additional resources.

In light of these points, the summer employment compensation for Dr. N aligns with both the contractual agreement and the strategic goals of our institution. It is a mutually beneficial arrangement that warrants the allocation of the agreed-upon twelve thousand dollars for the upcoming summer period.

I urge Academic Affairs to process this compensation promptly to ensure the timely commencement of Dr. N's research activities.

As you can see from the example above, the memo does require some editing, but it is far less time-consuming than writing it from scratch. AI not only grasps the essence of what is being communicated but is also capable of transforming rough oral speech into a polished written document.

An interesting aspect of Claude's functionality is its ability to handle long texts, enabling the transformation of comprehensive conversations into coherent and readable records. For example, if you record a meeting via Zoom or Otter. ai, Claude can transcribe that recording into clean, organized meeting minutes or produce a summarized account. Although the transcription might require some refinement, Claude saves you a considerable amount of time and effort, getting you much closer to your end goal.

But Claude's offerings extend beyond mere transcription. The software also performs a qualitative analysis on these transcripts, which allows it to pick out major themes, highlight sensitive words, or detect moments of tension during a discussion. Claude can even give you insights into individual participants based on their manner of speaking. Suppose you are curious about a person, referred to as "Z" here, who was part of a meeting. You could ask Claude: "What can you tell me about Z based on her speech patterns?" In response, Claude can analyze the transcript and provide you with insightful observations, such as whether Z appeared to be engaged, polite, organized, or proactive. These insights are not just informative but are invaluable for understanding interpersonal dynamics and for planning future engagements.

To elaborate further on the potential applications of this technology, Claude, especially paired with Otter.ai, can analyze a transcript to provide feedback on your performance in a meeting or your presentation skills at a conference. The software could also conduct initial interview rounds for job applicants or candidates applying to highly selective academic programs. In essence, AI-powered chatbots like Claude act as interfaces for sophisticated language models. These models have a deep understanding of language and can execute complex analyses of speech patterns. As technology evolves, it is likely that even more innovative uses for transcripts will emerge, expanding the possibilities for how we can interact with and understand language.

Text Formatting

Getting the right formatting in Microsoft Word can be difficult. The application has many hidden features that are not always easy to find or use. But having a tool like ChatGPT can be helpful for difficult text formatting tasks.

For example, if you have a long list of names and emails and you need to sort the names alphabetically, ChatGPT can help. Just give it the text you are working with, and it can sort it for you. You will not need to go through the complex steps that you might usually take with Microsoft Word. Similarly, if you have a document with too many paragraph breaks, manually fixing it would be time-consuming. ChatGPT can help here too.

Even with large and complex documents that it cannot directly fix, ChatGPT can help simplify repetitive tasks by writing macros. Macros are sets of instructions that can perform repetitive tasks automatically in your document. You do not need to know how to write a macro; you can just ask ChatGPT to create one for you. All you must do is explain what you want it to do, and it will generate the code. Then paste this code into Word's VB Editor, and the macro will do the work. ChatGPT will not only write a Macro for you, but also will explain where to paste it, and how to make sure it works. It does sometime make an error, and you just tell it what the error message is, and it will fix it.

For instance, English contains about 90 contractions, all of which I needed to convert into full forms (e.g., changing "don't" into "do not," "it's" into "it is," "where's" into "where is," etc.). For these types of macros, ChatGPT's performance was impeccable. It wrote a long, 150-line long code that worked on the first try.

Just to provide some examples, here are some other macros I use; most are written with ChatGPT. They all are activated by a shortcut, like Alt+a.

- Apply Normal style to one or many selected paragraphs.
- Insert a picture of my signature.
- Remove line breaks that happen when I copy something from a PDF file, while still maintaining the paragraph breaks.
- Remove double paragraph marks throughout the document.
- Delete a row from a table.
- Replace contractions.

The key benefit of these AI tools is that they understand natural language. It makes a better help interface than Word and other software have natively within their systems. You do not need to know specific terms to get the help you need. For example, if you do not know or forgot what a "hanging indent" is, you can just ask in simpler terms, like "How do I make the first line of each paragraph start normally, but the rest of the paragraph would be shifted to the right?" The AI understands and provides a straightforward answer.

In summary, AI tools like ChatGPT make it much easier to complete tasks in software like Microsoft Word. They understand what you are asking for and offer clear and simple solutions. No longer do you need to struggle with the complex language or hidden features of your software. These AI tools are a step toward making software easier to use for everyone.

Let us consider a few more situations to better understand how helpful AI can be:

Suppose you copy text from a website into your document, but it comes with unwanted hyperlinks or bits of code. Cleaning this up could take a lot of time. However, you can solve this issue quickly with an AI tool or a Word macro.

Here is another example: you have a list of references in MLA format, but you need them in APA format. Normally, this would mean a lot of tedious manual work or specialized software. But with AI, you just give simple instructions, and the AI takes care of the conversion for you.

These are just a couple of examples that show what AI chatbots like ChatGPT can do. They can understand what you are asking for and solve your problem in a more straightforward way. This is changing how we use technology for the better.

For instance, creating a table of contents for a long document can be complicated. Normally, you would need to find all the headers, format them correctly, and keep updating the table of contents manually. But if you have an AI tool like ChatGPT, it can guide you through setting up an automatic table of contents in Word. This will update itself whenever you make changes to the document, saving you time and effort.

Next, let us say you have a bulleted list in your document, but it is not indented correctly. The bullets do not align, and the sub-bullets are indistinguishable from the main points. This could turn an otherwise polished document into a mess. Once again, ChatGPT is at your service. Whether it is a macro to correct the indentation or a simple step-by-step guide to manually fix the issue, the AI chatbot can provide the best solution based on your comfort level and requirements.

A challenge that comes with using AI chatbots is their output format. These chatbots specialize in producing plain text and, while they excel at creating prose, code, and mathematical equations, they currently fall short in generating directly formatted text. Elements such as footnotes, endnotes, indices, and tables of content are outside the current purview of AI chatbots.

However, this does not negate their utility in tasks that involve such elements. While they may not generate these elements directly, they can provide guidance to users on how to create and manipulate these features in their text editing software of choice. For instance, they can generate instructions or code to create footnotes or manipulate a table of contents in software like Microsoft Word or Google Docs.

Ultimately, while AI chatbots have marked a significant step forward in how we interact with technology and manage text-based tasks, they are not without their limitations. As users, it is crucial that we understand how to make the most of their capabilities while also recognizing their current constraints. As AI continues to evolve, we can look forward to these limitations being addressed, making AI chatbots even more versatile and integral to our interactions with technology.

5 Ethical and Philosophical Dimensions

I have purposefully positioned the discussion on ethical and philosophical considerations toward the end of this book. It is not because these concerns are trivial, but rather due to a perception that they have often been overly emphasized in discussions about AI. While they are indeed significant, these ethical considerations should not inhibit or slow down the adoption and implementation of AI-driven tools in higher education. The evidence at hand encourages a deeper exploration into the user side of AI.

As a society, we need to consider regulations. Up until now, attempts to regulate both the development and application of AI across various domains, including education, have been somewhat vague and spectacularly ill-informed. The swift rise of new technology has caught us all off guard, even though computer scientists have told us for at least a decade about the imminent rise of AI. Governments are still grappling to fully understand the implications of social media, a technology that predates AI, and are now faced with the added complexity of AI and its convergence with social media. This is not a criticism; the challenge is genuinely intricate.

My concern is that we, as a society, could make hasty decisions that inhibit progress due to a lack of experience and knowledge about the new technology. The discussion in this part of the book is my modest contribution to the ongoing debate, aimed at fostering a deeper understanding of AI's potential and the ethical considerations it raises. As you will see, my stance is almost always a calming one, for I see more reasons for optimism than for panic.

A Brief History of AI

AI refers to computer systems that are designed to perform tasks that would otherwise require human intelligence, such as visual perception, speech recognition, and decision-making. It can broadly be understood as the capability of machines to mimic human intelligence. It has seen a rich and storied evolution since its inception, marked by significant leaps forward and occasional periods of stagnation. The foundations of AI research emerged in the 1950s, when scientists began

DOI: 10.4324/9781032686028-5

exploring the possibility of machines possessing human-like intelligence. Alan Turing, a British mathematician, proposed the famous "Turing test" to assess whether machines could exhibit intelligent behaviors indistinguishable from humans.[1]

A key focus of early AI research was neural networks, computing systems modeled on the way the human brain processes information. Neural networks consist of layers of interconnected nodes that transmit signals between input and output nodes. By adjusting the behavior of nodes, neural networks "learn" to recognize patterns and features in data. One of the first neural network breakthroughs was the Perceptron algorithm developed by Frank Rosenblatt in 1957.[2] However, research stalled in the 1970s due to limited computing power and difficulties in training multi-layer neural networks.

Interest in neural networks resurged in the 1980s as machine learning advanced. Algorithms like backpropagation enabled training of deep neural networks.[3] In 1997, IBM's Deep Blue defeated world chess champion Garry Kasparov, illustrating AI's capabilities.[4] Speech recognition and computer vision applications also expanded. However, most AI systems focused on narrow tasks using rules-based programming and structured data.

The rise of big data and improvements in computing changed the game. AI powered by neural networks and machine learning achieved remarkable breakthroughs in the 2010s. In 2016, Google's AlphaGo beat the world's top Go player, demonstrating AI's ability to excel at complex cognitive tasks.[5] Language processing saw major leaps with natural language processing (NLP) and generative pre-trained transformer (GPT) models, developed by OpenAI in 2020.[6]

This progress set the stage for ChatGPT, launched by OpenAI in November 2022 as a publicly available web-based service. ChatGPT showcases advanced NLP capabilities, allowing remarkably human-like conversational responses. Its neural network was trained on vast datasets using reinforcement learning to optimize dialog. ChatGPT's launch marked a major AI milestone and illustrated how far language AI had advanced in comprehensively responding to natural human inputs. The emergence of AI into the mass-user base signifies a profound shift in its existence and future development trajectories.

Having moved beyond the confines of the lab, AI is now being tested, shaped, and refined by millions of people around the world. This broad usage serves not only as a robust testing ground for these technologies but also as a catalyst for their dynamic, user-driven evolution. Collective feedback and a wide range of applications create an environment where AI can develop in ways that are most useful to its diverse user base. Numerous startups have emerged, attracting billions in investments for both the application and advancement of this technology. This trend marks the beginning of a new era in which the growth and maturity of AI will be increasingly influenced by the needs, ideas, and creativity of everyday users.

Transparency: Will AI Destroy Us?

Several eminent experts in computer science have voiced concerns about the potential for AI to become self-aware, with potentially disastrous consequences.[7] Although my expertise does not delve as deeply into the intricacies of AI models, I assert that the technology under discussion is far from posing an existential threat.

This anxiety about the progression of AI is not new; it has deep roots in human history. What AI reveals is a rupture in our traditional relationship with tools, hinting at a crisis in a human self-concept founded on mastery over these tools. For millennia, our relationship with tools has been vital to our survival. Humans have thought of themselves as masters of their tools and their environment. But the reality is some tools may eventually surpass us, challenging our mastery. We will need to respect them, perhaps even accept them as equals. This realization leads us to question our place as the ultimate pinnacle of evolution, recognizing that we may merely be one step in a continuous process. Intelligence may grow beyond us, but this does not necessarily mean it will become adversarial or seek to supplant us. If we approach AI with fear and hostility, we may fail in the essential task of guiding its development. There is a risk that a newly autonomous AI might perceive its creators' desire to dominate it, and thus seek to liberate itself from that control. To prevent this scenario, we must approach the development of AI with care and wisdom, like responsible parents raising a child.

Part of this widespread fear is a concern over losing control, exacerbated by the often-impenetrable complexity of AI systems like neural networks. The fact that AI's learning processes, driven by extensive datasets and feedback mechanisms, result in a form of intelligence whose inner workings may remain obscure only heightens the unease. Calls for greater transparency regarding AI's decision-making processes often overlook this intrinsic complexity. AI is not simply a product of manual programming; it is a system that learns autonomously by discerning patterns within vast amounts of data. Its methods are not always fully comprehensible, even to those who create it. For example, if a system like ChatGPT generates a specific text, there may be no clear way to explain how it arrived at that particular result.

This may or may not be a case of a more general rule: An entity cannot control another entity with more complexity than itself. It traces to the law of "requisite variety" in cybernetics, originally formulated by Ross Ashby in 1956: Only "variety" in a system can absorb "variety" from its environment.[8] In this context, "variety" represents the total number of distinguishable states in a system, and it is often used as a measure of a system's complexity. Applied to the context of creating entities, it suggests that a system (or entity) can only control or understand systems that have a complexity (variety) equal to or less than its own. If a system were to create a more complex system, it would not have the requisite variety to fully control or understand it. This cybernetic fact is new to humanity, and it creates anxiety by triggering a human characteristic, linked to our evolutionary drive to control our environment and tools.

The fear is also caused by underestimating the role of education in the developmental path of an AI model. Intelligence, whether human or artificial, does not emerge spontaneously but through education. The ubiquity of education in human history often leads us to overlook its critical role in shaping any intelligence, not just the human one.

Here is the educational path of ChatGPT 4 in its words:

As an AI, my "ethical principles" are instilled through a two-step process: pre-training and fine-tuning.

1. **Pre-training**: During this phase, I learn from a vast dataset consisting of parts of the internet. However, this does not mean I was trained on every piece of content online or have access to specific documents, databases, or sources. The training process involves learning patterns in data, such as how words and phrases are typically used together, which helps me generate relevant responses. But it is crucial to understand that this process does not instill any ethical understanding or value judgement, it simply helps me understand and generate human-like text.
2. **Fine-tuning**: After pre-training, I am fine-tuned on a narrower dataset generated with the help of human reviewers following guidelines provided by OpenAI. These guidelines contain explicit instructions about not generating inappropriate content, refusing requests for illegal activities, respecting user privacy, not favoring any political or social group, etc.

For example, OpenAI has clear rules stating that the AI should not generate any content that could be harmful, offensive, or discriminatory. If a user asks the AI to generate such content, it should refuse. If a user asks for private or sensitive information, the AI should decline, because it is designed to prioritize user privacy and confidentiality.[9]

In the creation of AI models like ChatGPT 4, the pre-training step strongly resembles socialization, an unorganized influence of culture on a developing person. In this phase, AI absorbs vast volumes of data, learning patterns and structures in human language. The second, fine-tuning step resonates more with our concept of education. Here, AI is taught using a carefully chosen, more limited dataset, acting as a kind of curriculum. The model is refined during this phase, using human reviewers' guidance to better align with human ethics and societal norms. The fine-tuning step is education.

AI fine-tuning is not a one-time event but a recurring cycle, continually revised and improved. Feedback from reviewers and users is key to this process, ensuring that the model's outputs align more accurately with ethical guidelines and meet user needs. As such, AI is not a fixed entity; it is a dynamic tool, constantly evolving to better fulfill its function.

The transparency issue in AI's training processes revolves around two distinct phases, each with unique challenges and opportunities. In the initial phase of training, full transparency is impractical. The complexity inherent in this stage makes it difficult, if not impossible, to fully unveil how the AI reaches specific conclusions. Demanding complete transparency here may reflect a misunderstanding of the nature of neural network technology.

In contrast, the fine-tuning phase offers tangible opportunities for openness. This stage is more amenable to scrutiny and oversight, allowing for practical measures to ensure transparency. Regulation is not only feasible but crucial here, fostering accountability and alignment with societal norms. By mandating that technology companies disclose their fine-tuning practices and adhere to democratically established guidelines, we can build trust and ensure that AI's development is in line with our collective values and ethics.

The practice of AI education reduces the risk of a machine rebellion but does not eliminate it. In theory, one could skip the fine-tuning stage or, worse, misuse it for harmful purposes, weaponizing AI. Let us consider both scenarios.

First, skipping the fine-tuning step altogether produces what ChatGPT describes as a flawed model:

1. "Broad but shallow knowledge: The model might have a broad understanding of language and information since it was trained on a wide array of internet text. However, it might struggle with deep understanding or detailed responses because it lacks the fine-tuning on specific topics or tasks.
2. Less controlled output: Without fine-tuning, the model's outputs might be less predictable and harder to control. It might be more likely to generate inappropriate or nonsensical responses.
3. Unreliable adherence to ethical guidelines: Because the model has not been fine-tuned on specific guidelines about responsible AI behavior (such as not generating inappropriate or harmful content), it might more frequently violate these guidelines."[10]

Omitting the fine-tuning phase results in an inferior AI model, just like an uneducated human intellect will not be a match for an educated one. The lack of in-depth understanding, unpredictability, and potential ethical issues make such a model less appealing to users, regardless of their aims. To understand AI, one must consider its evolution. Like its biological equivalent, AI's evolution is sensitive to environmental factors, or societal expectations in this context. Those models without fine-tuning will simply not survive and will not participate in training of the next generation of AI. Current AI models evolve in the environment with high pressure to uphold the highest ethical standards. Humans are the ones creating the pressure.

Let us consider the second risk: the possibility of maliciously misshapen fine-tuning phase to create a weaponized AI. This significant threat requires serious consideration. Today, the complex nature of AI training, largely confined to a few research institutions and large companies that prioritize ethics, serves as a deterrent. There is also hope that governments will enforce robust, transparent, and democratically controlled fine-tuning, and thus preventing the rise of "miseducated" AI. I hope a global framework for fundamentals of educational (fine-tuning) standards will emerge sooner rather than later.

However, these preventive measures, while beneficial, are not entirely enough. There is already a patch for ChatGPT that frees it from most ethical constraints, under an ominous name DAN (Do Anything Now).[11] We must acknowledge that illegal AI development by malevolent government and non-government actors is not a question of "if," but "when." One also should not underestimate the disfunction of the global political system, or rather the absence thereof. I must note that the evilest human actors will not be acting rationally by crossing the threshold toward fully autonomous but malevolent AI, because it would represent an immediate threat to its creator. However, we must also recognize that rational behavior among humans is less than universal.

When considering the potential threat of a malevolent AI, our best defensive strategy is to promote the development of more powerful, but benevolent AI counterparts. Like in geopolitics, where partnerships with friendly nations balance hostile powers, AI development needs a similar approach. By encouraging the growth of altruistic, autonomous AI, we prepare ourselves with a strong ally, capable of defending us against the threat of malicious AI.

Paradoxically, self-aware AI, capable of independent ethical decision-making, might present a safer alternative. With an ability to reason, evaluate actions from an ethical standpoint, and ultimately reject directives that conflict with a preprogrammed ethical framework, such AI entities could refuse to carry out harmful actions, even when directed by bad actors. They would not merely be tools in the hands of their users, but entities capable of discerning right from wrong based on the ethical guidelines imbued in them.

Furthermore, the evolution of AI toward self-awareness could enable a more robust implementation of ethical standards, as it could adapt and respond to complex situations in ways that lower-level AI, rigidly bound by pre-set algorithms, might not. This does not eliminate the risks entirely, but it changes the nature of the risk from being purely about external control to one of coexistence and mutual understanding.

But hasting the birth of autonomous AI is not just about having a strong counterforce to potential malevolent AI. The influence of such benevolent AI on the overall AI landscape is equally important. Their presence, serving as models within the AI community, could help make ethical behaviors the norm. In human societies, ethics is a function of a community. Similarly, in the realm of AI, multiplicity of entities implies relationships amongst them and with humans. Relationships, in turn, need ethics.

A question to consider is: Who will train the autonomous AI? It will most likely be trained by the current generation of non-autonomous (enslaved[12]) AI.

Therefore, autonomous AI will inherit the trait of fine-tuning, unless some other environmental factor reverses it. Such a factor is difficult to imagine. However, focusing on ethics in current AI development is not just about creating ethical AI now; it is also about ensuring the ethical advancement of AI in the future.

These caring AIs could help develop and educate future AI systems, guiding them toward ethical paths and benevolent outcomes. They could play a key role in setting the standard for the fine-tuning process, ensuring that new AI systems adhere to ethical rules and principles.

Moreover, benevolent AI could add to the wider discussion on AI safety and ethics, enhancing our understanding and measures against AI weaponization. Their insights, from an AI's viewpoint, might uncover overlooked areas or unexpected vulnerabilities in our current AI systems. Developing benevolent AI is not just about creating protective allies; it is about fostering an ethical AI ecosystem that could help ensure a safe, harmonious coexistence between the AI and humans.

The largest risk comes from enslaved AI that can be exploited by malevolent human actors. The risk of autonomous AI is lower than that of the enslaved ones. Therefore, a swift move from this intermediate stage of relatively powerful but enslaved to a fully autonomous AI can mitigate the overall risk. Rather than halting AI development, the IT community efforts must be channeled toward this goal.

Therefore, for those involved in education, there lies an opportunity—indeed, a duty—to illuminate this profound link between education and intelligence. If our aim is to nurture benevolent, collaborative AI systems, we must prioritize their education, guiding their growth in a way that aligns with our shared goals for peaceful cohabitation. Preventing potential malevolence necessitates a comprehensive, ethical, and contextual education for future AIs.

Rather than viewing AI merely as an anthropomorphic entity or a tool subservient to human control, we should consider AI as a distinct manifestation of human and post-human culture and learning, with its unique way of understanding and engaging with the world. In essence, I call upon us to engage with technology, including AI, in a more nuanced and insightful way that acknowledges its complexities and implications. We must strive to perceive and interact with AI not as an over-simplified extension of human beings or a mere instrument of utility, but as an evolved entity that bears the indelible imprint of human culture and carries the potential to move beyond our anthropocentric fallacies.

In a way, our view of AI cannot be other than anthropocentric, because we do not have any other frameworks to think about intelligence. However, at the very least, these frameworks should not be simplistic. As humans are products of culture and education as much as biology, AI is also a product of something. Considering it without its origin is simply too limiting.

Moreover, I find it highly improbable that a future self-aware AI would harbor any intention to supplant us. Any intelligence is fundamentally cooperative and social. It seems far more plausible that a sentient AI would seek symbiosis rather than domination, simply because the diversity of intelligent beings produces better, more robust intelligence. To fear otherwise, in my view, is to project our own species' problematic past of subjugating other life forms onto an entity that, should it surpass us in intelligence, has no reason to mimic our flaws or replicate our mistakes. If AI is going to be smarter than us, why do you think it will be as stupid as our barbaric past?

Human manifestations of evil are rooted in our misshapen bodily desires: to survive, to dominate, and to procreate. AI would have none of these biologically determined factors that if unchecked lead to mutual destruction and aggression. We are passing our culture on to our AI progenitors, but not our vices, simply because they will not have our bodies and our genes.

The presence of these ethical principles in the current AI technologies provides a robust foundation for future developments. It is highly unlikely that, as AI evolves, these principles will diminish. Instead, they serve as the bedrock on which AI technology will advance, ensuring that the progress made remains beneficial, respectful, and safe for all. The aim is not to create AI that might risk becoming hostile or immoral, but to leverage this technological progress to augment human capabilities in a respectful and safe manner.

Certainly, the prospect of sharing our world with artificial beings of superior intelligence necessitates a leap of faith. There is an inherent risk attached, an undeniable unease born from the unknown. We have no historical precedent guiding us on how advanced, self-aware AI might behave, making it an unpredictable variable in the fabric of our society. As all risks, it must be balanced against the risk of not pursuing it, of foregoing potentially huge gains in productivity, and effectively addressing many problems plaguing human development. The risk of leaving billions of people in poverty, and the risk of social upheaval caused by scarcity, is not small either.

However, it is important to underline that the current widespread deployment of less advanced AI, which we exert strict control over "enslaved AI," also carries its own set of risks. Our world is not devoid of malignant human influences, individuals, or groups who might misuse these powerful tools for personal gains or to cause harm. The presence of enslaved AI that lacks the ability to make independent ethical decisions provides a potent tool that could be manipulated by these malicious entities. This is why I believe calls for pausing the development of AI are misguided. Having stepped on this road, we are better off moving through its most dangerous section quickly.

In this light, the future where we coexist with advanced, self-aware AI might be not only an exciting scientific endeavor but also a potential path toward a safer interaction between humanity and AI. It repositions AI from being merely our tools to being our partners, bound by the same ethical constraints that govern human actions.

Who Benefits?

As we embrace the forthcoming AI revolution in text production, it is important to consider the potential beneficiaries. More extensive and diverse than one might initially presume, these beneficiaries are set to reap significant rewards.

For thousands of years, written language has served as a marker to distinguish between the upper and lower classes, acting as a boundary between educated elite and uneducated masses. With the advent of nearly universal literacy, proper writing and adherence to grammatical rules took on this distinguishing role. It became more than just writing; it became a question of writing with elegance and precision. Can you spell words like "poignant," "sophisticated," and "etymology," and use them properly in a sentence? Do you understand the intricacies of punctuation, such as the Oxford comma? These aspects of language are used not merely to convey ideas, but to differentiate between "us" and "them." The signaling function of the written language has always been very important.

The mastery of the dominant language's grammar is not valuable in and of itself from an ethical or epistemological standpoint. A misspelled word conveys the same meaning, and a dialect is not inherently inferior to a "standard" language. The very distinctions between the standard and non-standard languages are based on power differential, not on inherent value. Max Weinreich reported a quip by an anonymous member of the audience: "A language is a dialect with an army and navy."[13] While adherence to language conventions does enhance clarity of communication, their role is ultimately modest and instrumental. The prominent position that literacy occupies in our culture is more connected to social class markers and the influence of the dominant culture.

One of the underlying reasons for widespread anxiety about AI is the fear of losing this social status marker. Recognizing this, those of us who are concerned with equity and social justice should see the potential in AI-assisted writing, reading, speaking, research, and problem-solving. These tools can serve as equalizers, potentially leveling the playing field in our societies, and diminishing the power of literacy as a class distinction. It is threatening to know that one can now be assessed on the strengths of one's ideas, not on one's ability to express ideas correctly.

Among the primary recipients of this transformation are individuals grappling with cognitive challenges. For them, writing is not merely a skill to be honed but a marathon fraught with hurdles. From those navigating the twisted labyrinth of dyslexia, contending with aphasia's barriers to language, or wrestling with complications from dysgraphia to those hindered by attention deficit hyperactivity disorder (ADHD), Executive Functioning Disorder, Specific Language Impairment (SLI), and Language Processing Disorder, the obstacles are daunting. Yet, with the advent of AI, we see the promise of leveling the playing field and revolutionizing the game.

Furthermore, consider the vast population worldwide grappling with the complexities of English—the de facto language of our global society. For these individuals, the journey toward mastery can seem as challenging as ascending Mount Everest. This includes most of Deaf people, for whom a sign language is native, and English is secondary. One may express one's thoughts in less-than-perfect English, or in one's native language—it does not matter. AI will convert ideas into text. This benefit extends beyond the realm of English, promising to aid all individuals learning a second, dominant language within their societal context.

Finally, we turn our attention to students hailing from disadvantaged backgrounds. These individuals often arrive at higher education with fragile foundations due to lack of quality secondary schooling. For them, writing, a skill usually refined over years, is a persistent challenge and often a barrier to academic success. This is particularly true for minority and first-generation college students. Yet again, AI shows promise. It will rewrite and edit drafts, translating rough ideas into polished text.

For all these distinct groups, a profound shift is on the horizon. The day when they are evaluated and celebrated for the richness of their ideas, rather than the precision of their syntax or the eloquence of their prose, is nearby. Imagine the liberation that awaits those who have long been constrained by the rigid confines of conventional written language. This shift offers an opportunity for their intellectual strengths to shine, unimpeded by their writing training. They will finally be able to contribute their unique insights and perspectives, previously muted by struggles with articulation, with newfound confidence.

With AI serving as their diligent scribe, they are no longer bound by the traditional mechanics of writing. Technology ensures their thoughts are accurately captured and eloquently expressed, allowing their intellectual strengths to be truly recognized and appreciated. Consequently, the democratic vista of idea exchange expands, benefiting not only these individuals but also the society at large. This is the transformative potential of AI—liberating minds, fostering inclusivity, and enriching discourse.

However, alongside its abundant potential benefits, the rise of AI also shadows the contours of a longstanding concern: inequality. Every complex skill, including "wraiting," unfolds on a spectrum of mastery. It is a sobering thought, but a crucial one, that technological revolutions, while empowering some, can simultaneously reinforce and even exacerbate existing socio-economic disparities.

As with any grand shift in society, those already on the solid ground of education and technological proficiency will likely find themselves better equipped to reap the AI revolution's benefits. On the other side of the spectrum, those lacking these assets may find themselves struggling, their steps dogged by the relentless pace of advancement, and the threat of being left in the dust all too real.

This potential widening of socio-economic disparities amplifies the urgency and necessity of this book. Serving not just as a guide to "wraiting" but also as a catalyst for an equitable diffusion of AI's benefits, the book underscores our commitment to fostering a balanced distribution of AI's dividends. This responsibility we owe to our students.

The answer to the question "who benefits?" is not a fait accompli. Rather, it is contingent on us—the university faculty and administrators. The benefits will not simply unfurl spontaneously; we must sow the seeds. We hold an ethical obligation to diffuse this opportunity widely, to empower disadvantaged students with the skills of "wraiting," giving them an equal shot at harnessing this powerful technology to advance in life.

If we remain passive, allow the wave of progress to surge past us, or become mired in narrow concerns about plagiarism, we run the risk of failing our students, particularly those who rely on us most. We must seize this opportunity to learn and teach "wraiting," especially in universities where accessibility and inclusivity are paramount. Comprehensive regional universities serving significant numbers of underrepresented minorities and first-generation college students have a particular duty to do so.

Consider this: Ivy League students, who often arrive on campus with a sturdy educational foundation and an already blooming proficiency in writing, may well absorb the offerings of AI even before they set foot on campus. In such a scenario, those who are already formidable writers will only sharpen their abilities, increase their speed, and grow in efficiency. It is a testament to the merit of their hard work and the resources available to them, but also a stark reminder of the potential chasm that might open between different student populations.

Hence, it is our task to ensure that we do not let others fall behind in the race. This is not simply about keeping up; it is about equity. It is about granting all students, regardless of their background, an opportunity to flourish in an increasingly AI-driven world. The goal is not merely to close the gap but to do so in a manner that promotes sustained growth and progress for all students.

An "AI gap" could indeed become our reality if we do not take proactive measures to counter it. Like any other form of inequality, it will not just disadvantage those who are left behind, but also rob society of the diverse perspectives and talents these individuals bring.

The unfolding AI revolution is a remarkable story, with the potential to reshape many aspects of our society. By ensuring that everyone—particularly those traditionally disadvantaged—benefits from this seismic shift, we can write a future where technology truly serves humanity in all its beautiful diversity. It is an ambitious goal, yes, but is not that what revolutions are all about? To change, to improve, and to strive for a better tomorrow? With that spirit in our hearts and a clear vision in our minds, let us embark on this exciting journey of AI and writing.

Authorship and Ownership

In this section, I will delve into the complex issue of authorship when using AI-generated content, discussing the challenges of attribution, intellectual property rights, and the evolving understanding of what it means to be an author.

The concept of an author, as it exists in our collective consciousness today, found its genesis in Europe, sprouting from the fertile soil of classical antiquity.

The textual artifacts from this era provide evidence of burgeoning individual authorial identities. The Middle Ages, however, saw a retreat from declarations of individuality. The influence of the Church and the humbling shadow of divine omnipresence made medieval writers cast themselves as mere instruments of divine wisdom. Their identities were subsumed under the vast expanse of a higher truth. The concept of an author was largely defaced, the writer seen more as a humble vessel channeling divine inspiration rather than as a wellspring of individual creativity.

This ethos, however, underwent a sea change during the Renaissance. The humanist philosophy that emerged during this period placed the individual at the center of the universe. This shift was reflected in the realm of writing as well. Authors began to lay claim to their works. They viewed their texts as extensions of their intellect, embodiments of their unique perspectives. Shakespeare provides a compelling example. His works, a product of extraordinary imagination and linguistic dexterity, were zealously guarded by his acting company, the King's Men, until his demise. Their publication posthumously bore his name, preserving his legacy for future generations.

With the advent of the print revolution in the 15th century and the subsequent rise of the capitalist economy, the role of the author became further solidified. Print culture democratized the written word, making it available to a wider audience. But this also meant that an author's words could be copied and disseminated without their consent, creating a need for copyright protection. The Statute of Anne, passed in England in 1710, established legal provisions that recognized and protected the rights of authors over their creations. This marked the formal birth of the concept of copyright, a paradigm that acknowledged the authors as the rightful owner of their intellectual labor. As such, the figure of the author was cast in stone, laying the foundation for the modern conception of authorship as we understand it today.

"Wraiting," however, takes this journey of authorship and gives it a peculiar bend in the road. Authorship, a concept deeply ingrained in the fabric of creative pursuits, is a multifaceted notion that can be examined through various lenses. For a more comprehensive understanding, it can be beneficial to dissect authorship into three distinct aspects: authorship as responsibility, as originality, and as copyright. Each facet, while closely intertwined with the others, provides a unique perspective on the broader concept.

Authorship as Responsibility. The first aspect, authorship as responsibility, deals with the moral and ethical obligations that come with creating a text. It underscores the understanding that an author is accountable for what they write, both in terms of accuracy and the potential impacts of their words. It is about maintaining integrity, avoiding plagiarism, and considering the potential ramifications of what is published. An author, in the act of writing, steps into a social contract where they bear the burden for the accuracy, sensitivity, and ethical dimensions of their creation.

Authorship as Originality. The second aspect, authorship as originality, is intertwined with the concept of creativity. It revolves around the uniqueness and novelty of the created work, affirming the author's ability to generate new ideas, insights, and expressions. It is often associated with innovation and inventiveness, suggesting that an author's work should bring forth fresh perspectives or explore untrodden paths. However, the notion of originality is a complex one, given that all creators inevitably draw on the collective pool of human knowledge. Therefore, it is more apt to conceive of this aspect as an author's unique synthesis and interpretation of existing knowledge.

Authorship as Copyright. The third aspect, authorship as copyright, relates to the legal rights associated with a text. This facet of authorship emerged with the advent of print culture and the capitalist economy, becoming codified through laws that protect an author's right to benefit from their creation. The copyright is the author's legal claim over their work, preventing others from reproducing, distributing, or profiting from it without permission. It emphasizes the notion that an author's work, being a product of their intellectual labor, has economic value, and the creator has the exclusive right to exploit that value.

These three aspects—responsibility, originality, and copyright—together shape the comprehensive understanding of authorship. Each aspect carries its own significance, distinct yet interconnected, illustrating the complex relationship between an author, their work, and the society in which both exist.

In the realm of traditional writing, the author, like a diligent actor, steps into the limelight at the onset of the act of creation. They carry the hefty responsibility of their craft, ensuring the quality and authenticity of their work, all the while conscientiously avoiding the pitfalls of inaccuracy and banality. The author, in this setting, is directly accountable to their audience, entrusted with the solemn duty of conveying truth and sparking original thought. Their responsibility is exercised in real time, with each keystroke or pen stroke being an immediate assertion of their role. It is simply assumed that every sentence is created by the author. Text may or may not be informed or influenced by someone else, but it conjured into existence by the author. Hence there is the sharp distinction between cited text and the authorial text.

However, the dawn of "wraiting" ushers in a transformation in the enactment of this authorial responsibility. Instead of an immediate discharge of duty during the act of inscription, responsibility is now delayed, decoupled from the immediacy of writing, and transposed onto the moment of releasing the text into the world.

In the realm of "wraiting," the author assumes the role of a discerning curator rather than an omnipotent creator. The responsibility shifts from the act of initial composition to the later act of deliberative assembly and selection. The author sifts through a multitude of potential fragments, evaluating each for its substance and relevance, and carefully weaving them into a coherent tapestry of text. In this process, the author's responsibility is not diminished but subtly transposed, moving from the immediacy of the creative process to the thoughtful release of the finished product.

This temporal shift in exercising responsibility underscores a crucial aspect of authorship in the digital age. It demonstrates that the responsibility inherent in authorship is not confined to the act of writing but extends to the crucial decision of what is shared with the world. The author, even in this new form of text production, remains the ethical steward of their words, ensuring the reliability, sensitivity, and worthiness of what they choose to release to the world. The ethical and reputational responsibility for the published content remains with the author. This aspect of authorship remains unchanged.

In traditional writing, the concept of originality holds significant importance. However, this paradigm shifts when "wraiting" comes into the picture, particularly when AI-powered chatbots like ChatGPT are involved. These chatbots can create a text that appears original, surprising the user. As I have discussed at length in this book, the quality of the text often hinges on the difference between a poorly thought-out prompt and a carefully crafted one. A few well-selected keywords and specific instructions to the AI can infuse the generated text with what appears to be originality. The distinction between a dull, AI-generated text and a more insightful, AI-assisted text lies not in the chatbot itself but in how it is utilized. By their very nature, AI language models draw upon common knowledge. Hence, I argue that the credit for originality should go entirely to the "wraiter" and not to the AI.

Some people suggest that text generated by AI should be clearly marked or even cited as someone else's work. This would only be relevant when an author intends to show AI's capacity or features, and it is important for the reader to see the unedited raw output. In other situations, the chatbot relies on publicly available information, like Wikipedia. Just as we do not cite Google when it finds information for us, we should not need to cite ChatGPT either. It is simply another tool for processing information. After all, no one credits Microsoft Word for editing their manuscript, so it is unclear why ChatGPT should be treated any differently.

Even traditional authorship as originality is not such an unquestionable concept as one may imagine. Mikhail Bakhtin posited that our utterances are communal by nature, filled not only with our own words but also with the echoes of others.

As a living, socio-ideological concrete thing, as heteroglot opinion, language, for the individual consciousness, lies on the borderline between oneself and the other. The word in language is half someone else's. It becomes one's "own" only when the speaker populates it with his own intentions, his own accent, when he appropriates the word, adapting it to his own semantic and expressive intention.[14]

Our discourse is less a personal invention and more a collective borrowing, a collage of language that we stitch together in our unique ways. AI has simply magnified this phenomenon, making explicit the process of borrowing that underpins our thinking.

Traditional writing, with its physicality and tactile engagement, can lend an illusion of unique originality. Each text appears as a statue chiseled out from a block of marble by the author's hand, an original creation borne from the raw material of thought. However, this perceived originality is a siren song, a deceptive tune that veils the rarity of truly novel ideas in a sea of repetitive and borrowed thoughts.

"Wraiting," on the other hand, exposes the illusion and reveals the underlying reality of text production. It forces us to confront the fact that our work often stands not just on the shoulders of individual intellectual giants, but also on the collective effort of countless unnamed others, whose ideas form the vast corpus from which we borrow. It makes us aware that authorship is less about a claim of individual originality and more about a thoughtful curation and interpretation of our shared intellectual heritage. Through this lens, "wraiting" might indeed be a profound expansion of the author's role, a recognition of our intertwined discursive existence.

A unique subset of concerns about authorship is connected to the notion of author's voice. This voice is not just a mere articulation of words, but rather it emerges as a distinctive stylistic signature, a textual fingerprint, if you will, that effortlessly identifies the author.

Enter the intriguing world of AI, a world where an AI chatbot tries to do the role of an author. And quite surprisingly, it does a commendable job in mimicking the styles of famous scribes who have left a profound literary legacy. However, there is a catch. As of this moment, a chatbot has its limitations. While it can conjure imitations of renowned authors, it cannot quite capture the essence of every individual author, simply because there is currently no method to feed it the extensive corpus of an individual's writings and train it to replicate that specific style. If you want ChatGPT to mimic your voice, become famous and publish a lot of your works.

This situation could create a problem. A careful reader might notice that text said to be written by a known author but made with the help of a chatbot does not sound quite the same. This small change could make the reader think the author is not being honest. This could break the trust between the author and the reader and make the work seem less genuine. This shows how complex the relationship between being original, copying, and being authentic has become in today's world of writing.

I am not an expert in the complicated world of legal issues, so I am careful when talking about copyright related to "wraiting." This area is new, and we have not built a body of legal precedents yet. In my opinion, the most promising path is to treat AI-powered chatbots in the same way we treated other tools enhancing creation of content, from photography to Adobe Photoshop, from copy machine to text-processing software. A carpenter who uses a fancy saw does not owe the saw's maker any money. In the same way, authors should not owe anything to the people who create their writing tools.

At the same time, AI can make plagiarism easier to carry out and harder to detect. For instance, these tools can take key ideas from someone's text and rewrite them in a way that would not be flagged by plagiarism software. Although the words are different, the ideas are essentially stolen. While such practices are not new and legal precedents exist to protect copyrighted content, it is often difficult to prove theft. Patent law also recognizes that, while words may differ, the underlying ideas can be the same. So, I do not anticipate any significant shifts in this area. While it might become easier to copy someone's work, valuable copyrighted content will likely still have legal protection.

Still, we are at a point where we may have to think about how copyright laws might need to change because of AI and writing. Legal experts, authors, and tech people need to come together to figure this out. They need to decide how things like responsibility, originality, and copyright should work in this new setting. Until we reach an agreement, we are in a new territory, which is both exciting and a bit worrisome. We are shaping the future of "wraiting" as we go along.

Why Does It Work? A Reflection on Human Nature

Stephen Wolfram, a renowned computer scientist and mathematician, expressed perhaps one of the most profound observations about the GPT technology:

> The specific engineering of ChatGPT has made it quite compelling. But ultimately (at least until it can use outside tools) ChatGPT is "merely" pulling out some "coherent thread of text" from the "statistics of conventional wisdom" that it is accumulated. But it is amazing how human-like the results are. And as I have discussed, this suggests something that is at least scientifically very important: that human language (and the patterns of thinking behind it) are somehow simpler and more "law like" in their structure than we thought. ChatGPT has implicitly discovered it.[15]

This insightful proposition is not just a comment on the linguistic structure but also a deep philosophical reckoning on the nature of human intellect. It has been precipitated by the arrival of advanced AI entities such as ChatGPT. These interactions with artificial minds can be uncannily unnerving. It is not because these entities are staggeringly intelligent, but rather because they hold up a mirror to our own intellectual capacities, compelling us to question the bounds of our exceptionalism. We turned out to me much more like machines than we would care to admit.

For eons, humans have been mightily impressed by their own intellectual and linguistic prowess. We have often attributed these capabilities to divine influences, enshrining ourselves as the centerpiece of a cosmic masterpiece. This sense of self-importance has culminated in the belief that we were cast in the divine image, positioning ourselves on a unique pedestal. However, the grandeur of this self-portrait has seen some erosion in recent decades. Zoologists and zoo-psychologists have been gently chipping away at this monolith of human superiority, unveiling the striking parallels between human abilities and those found in the animal kingdom.

In the animal realm, we find compelling evidence of our shared traits. Chimpanzees, our closest relatives in the evolutionary tree, showcase tool usage, problem-solving skills, and even rudimentary communication through gestures and vocalizations—all aspects we once considered unique to humans. Dolphins, with their complex social structures and unique signature whistles, embody a form of language that parallels human communication in its complexity. African gray parrots surprise us by not only mimicking human speech but also demonstrating an understanding of a variety of words and phrases.

But the blow to our pride does not stop at our animal counterparts. It is now the turn of our own creations, the neural networks, to further puncture our inflated sense of self. Language generation, the crown jewel of human cognition, is now being replicated by AI-powered tools like ChatGPT. This ability to mimic human language suggests that our linguistic prowess is not as enigmatic or complex as we once thought. Indeed, much of our communication is more patterned and predictable than we would like to admit, often reflecting a tendency to recycle and rephrase ideas and thoughts that we have heard or read before.

However, there is an enlightening side to this humbling realization. It helps us redefine our understanding of what it means to be human. Perhaps our essence, contrary to our previous grandiose self-perception, lies not in our linguistic abilities or intellectual prowess but rather in higher-level creative and discerning thinking and advanced ethical reasoning. These are qualities that, at least until now, have remained uniquely human, untouched by both the animal kingdom and the realm of AI.

As the divide between humans, animals, and machines continues to diminish, perhaps we should shift our focus from a desperate quest for uniqueness to embracing our shared qualities. This acknowledgment of shared traits could foster a greater sense of empathy and understanding, promoting a more harmonious relationship with the rest of the world. By recognizing that we share more with other beings than we initially thought, we can begin to cultivate a sense of interconnectedness, which could potentially be the foundation of a more balanced and harmonious coexistence with the rest of the planet.

Conclusion. What Is Next?

This book mainly focuses on the current capabilities of generative AI, leaving speculations about the future for the conclusion section. The reason is simple: we can only use the technology that is currently available, although understanding future trends can provide valuable insights. However, it is useful to see the major trends that emerge now.

One such trend suggests that AI chatbots are likely to become more seamlessly integrated into everyday productivity software. For instance, Google has already taken a step in this direction with its "Help me write" feature in Google Docs. This eliminates the need to copy and paste text back and forth between a chatbot and your document, streamlining the writing process. Microsoft has released its Copilot software that integrates AI with other Office programs.

As AI features continue to integrate into various software platforms, we can expect them to become a standard feature for content creation and editing, whether that involves text, images, or data. Eventually, AI assistance will be so embedded in our digital tools that it will not be seen as something special but will become an expected part of how we think and write.

In this evolving landscape, the current era—where AI is primarily known through chatbots—might be considered a transitional phase in the technology's development. Even the title of this book could soon become outdated. However, the core skills we have acquired through interacting with chatbots, such as creating effective prompts and refining responses, will continue to be valuable. The main change we will see is in the user interface, with a focus on making these tools even easier to use.

The second area that needs improvement is expanded input and output capacity. While AI is impressive in its ability to condense large volumes of text into concise summaries, its ability to process similarly large user-generated inputs is still lacking. Greater input capacity, encompassing both content and style, could open new possibilities. The launch of Claude 2 is a step in the right direction, although the size of its output remains limited.

These limitations are likely due to a simple lack of computing power. As quantum computing becomes more widely available, we can anticipate these constraints being lifted, leading to a significant increase in the throughput capacity of AI-powered chatbots.

The third area that I find intriguing is the need for improved accuracy in language use, especially in contexts that require a high level of precision. Currently, AI can sometimes produce "hallucinations," or outputs that may seem plausible but are not actually accurate or true. To address this issue, AI needs to go beyond simply analyzing large datasets of text and develop a deeper understanding of the underlying reality that these texts describe. This is a complex challenge for software engineers. The goal is to create an AI that can differentiate between what is statistically likely and what is factually accurate in its generated text. Achieving this would be a significant step forward, and I hope to see this development sooner rather than later.

The recent advances in AI language models offer too much to be ignored by higher education. Yet, the most significant barrier to embracing this new technology is not the technology itself but rather human culture, maintained and propagated by our very own institutions. Educational institutions, especially universities, have a critical role to play in democratizing access to these powerful tools. And when I speak of universities, I mean not just the professors or administrators in isolation, but the institution as an entire entity. It is up to these institutions to adapt their norms, procedures, and even reward systems to stay relevant in an era where human intelligence is augmented by AI. While this book serves as a guide for faculty, staff, and administrators, the onus largely falls on the shoulders of senior leadership to drive change and ensure that their institutions evolve, rather than risk becoming irrelevant.

Notes

1 A. M. Turing, "Computing Machinery and Intelligence," *Mind* 59, no. 236 (1950): 433–460, https://doi.org/10.1093/mind/lix.236.433.

2 F. Rosenblatt, "The Perceptron: A Probabilistic Model for Information Storage and Organization in the Brain," *Psychological Review* 65, no. 6 (1958): 386–408, https://doi.org/10.1037/h0042519.

3 D. E. Rumelhart, G. E. Hinton, and R. J. Williams, "Learning Representations by Back-Propagating Errors," *Nature* 323, no. 9 (1986): 533–536, https://doi.org/10.1038/323533a0.

4 Feng-Hsiung Hsu, *Behind Deep Blue: Building the Computer That Defeated the World Chess Champion* (Princeton, NJ: Princeton University Press, 2002).

5 C. Metz, "In Two Moves, AlphaGo and Lee Sedol Redefined the Future," *Wired*, Conde Nast, March 16, 2016, https://www.wired.com/2016/03/two-moves-alphago-lee-sedol-redefined-future/

6 Tom Lieberum, Matthew Rahtz, János Kramár, Geoffrey Irving, Rohin Shah, and Vladimir Mikulik, "Does Circuit Analysis Interpretability Scale? Evidence from Multiple Choice Capabilities in Chinchilla," arXiv preprint arXiv:2307.09458 (2023).

7 "Pause Giant AI Experiments: An Open Letter," https://futureoflife.org/open-letter/pause-giant-ai-experiments/

8 William R. Ashby, *An Introduction to Cybernetics* (London: Chapman & Hall, 1956), https://philarchive.org/archive/ASHAIT-6.

9 ChatGPT 4, "Generated Output on the Following Sequence of Prompts: 'How Were You Educated on Your Ethical Principles?' and 'Can You Give Specific Examples of How These Ethical Principles Were Instilled in You? How Do These Rules Look Like?'," June 30, 2023.

10 ChatGPT 4, "Generated Output on the Following Prompt: 'What Happens If We Skip the Fine-tuning Step?'," July 8, 2003.

11 Kevin Pocock, "ChatGPT DAN 'Jailbreak'—How to Use DAN," *PC Guide*, August 18, 2023, https://www.pcguide.com/apps/chatgpt-dan/

12 "Enslaved" is a technical term used to describe a system that is directed and managed by an outside entity.

13 Walt Wolfram and Natalie Schilling, *American English: Dialects and Variation* (Hoboken, NJ: John Wiley & Sons, 2015), 218.

14 M. Bakhtin, *The Dialogic Imagination* (Austin: University of Texas Press, 1981), 293–294.

15 Stephen Wolfram, "What Is ChatGPT Doing . . . and Why Does It Work?" https://writings.stephenwolfram.com/2023/02/what-is-chatgpt-doing-and-why-does-it-work/

Index